EXPERIENCE
ST. MAARTEN/ST. MARTIN,
ST. BARTH, AND ANGUILLA

D01258835

16 ULTIMATE EXPERIENCES

St. Maarten/St. Martin, St. Barth, and Anguilla offer terrific experiences that should be on every traveler's list. Here are Fodor's top picks for a memorable trip.

1 Shoal Bay, Anguilla

This 2-mile-long beach has powdery-soft sand and breathtaking turquoise water, making it one of the best of many beautiful beaches on the tiny island of Anguilla. *(Ch. 5)*

2 Loterie Farm, St. Martin

Zipline or hike at this family-friendly nature reserve and you'll be rewarded with views of Pic Paradis, the highest mountain on the island. Then, relax at the farm's cabana-lined pool. *(Ch. 3)*

3 Shopping, St. Barth

Even if you're just window-shopping, St. Barth is the Caribbean's ultimate destination for brand names and high-end boutiques, especially on Quai de la Republique in Gustavia. *(Ch. 4)*

4 Lunch at the Lolos, St. Martin

Some of the best dining bargains (and barbecue) in St. Martin can be found at outdoor roadside grills in Grand Case, the French side's culinary capital. *(Ch. 3)*

5 Elvis's Beach Bar, Anguilla

You can have one of the best rum punches in the Caribbean at this bar, which was made from a beached boat. Nothing beats being here with your feet in the sand during sunset. *(Ch. 5)*

6 Marigot, St. Martin

St. Martin's lovely seaside French capital has greatly recovered from Hurricane Irma thanks to the resiliency of its people. Don't miss its bustling harbor, streetside cafés, and boutiques. *(Ch. 3)*

7 Junior's Glass Bottom Boat, Anguilla

Junior Fleming and his glass-bottom boat are a bona fide Anguilla institution. The glass bottom is perfect for watching sea life without getting wet but you can also jump in and snorkel. *(Ch. 5)*

8 Golf at CuisinArt, Anguilla

A must for any serious golfer, this 18-hole course designed by Greg Norman has amazing views, with 13 out of 18 holes right on the water. *(Ch. 5)*

9 Ziplining in St. Maarten / St. Mar

Fly high over the Dutch side with the steepest vertical drop in the world at Rainforest Adventures' Rockland Estate. *(Ch. 3)*

10 Little Bay, Anguilla

Jump off "the Rock" at Little Bay beach, accessible only by boat or by scampering down a rope to the beach from the hill. There are two hills, one a bit taller than the other. *(Ch. 5)*

11 Maho Beach, St. Maarten

Watching planes land ridiculously low over your head at Maho Beach (or watching the people watching the planes) is one of the most popular activities in Dutch St. Maarten. *(Ch. 3)*

12 Baie Orientale, St. Martin

With beach bars and restaurants back and better than ever after Hurricane Irma, this beach is a lively scene once again. The southern end of the beach is clothing-optional. *(Ch. 3)*

13 Dune Preserve, Anguilla

Caribbean reggae artist Bankie Banx created this unforgettable musical oasis not far from the CuisinArt Golf Resort. Order a bite to eat and relax with your toes in the sand. *(Ch. 5)*

14 Anse de Grande Saline, St. Barth

Pounding surf, undeveloped shoreline, and an absence of facilities make this pristine beach feel wild, in the best way. Its seclusion makes it a natural choice for nudists. *(Ch. 4)*

15 Hotel Le Toiny Restaurant, St. Barth

Located high above Anse Toiny on St. Barth's Southeastern coast, the Hotel Le Toiny Restaurant is one of the island's premier dining destinations. The view is one of the best on the island. *(Ch. 4)*

16 Sundown in Philipsburg, St. Maarten

After a long day of duty-free shopping and lounging on the beach, grab a drink and watch the colors change over this bustling port. *(Ch. 3)*

WHAT'S WHERE

1 St. Maarten/St. Martin. Two nations (Dutch and French), many nationalities, one small island, a lot of development. But there are also more white, sandy beaches than days in a month. Go for the awesome restaurants, extensive shopping, and wide range of activities. Don't go if you're not willing to get out and search for the really good stuff.

2 St. Barthélemy. If you come to St. Barth for a taste of European village life, not for a conventional full-service resort experience, you will be richly rewarded. Go for excellent dining and wine, great boutiques with the latest hip fashions, world-class people-watching, and an active, on-the-go vacation. Don't go for big resorts, and make sure your credit card is platinum-plated.

3 Anguilla. With miles of brilliant white sand and accommodations that range from funky guest houses to elegant super-luxury resorts, Anguilla is a laid-back beach lover's heaven. Go for fine cuisine in elegant surroundings, great snorkeling, family-friendliness, and the funky late-night music scene. This island is all about relaxing and reviving. Don't go for shopping and sightseeing.

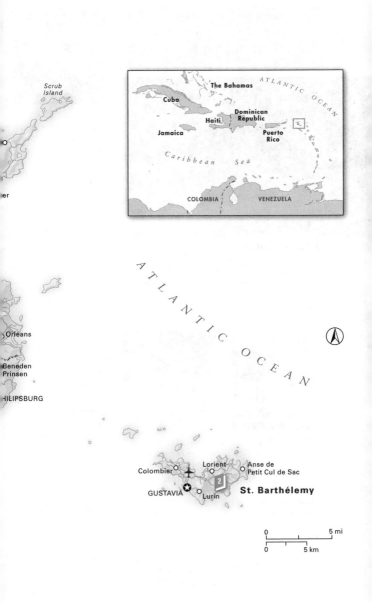

Scrub
Island

Orléans

Beneden
Prinsen

PHILIPSBURG

ATLANTIC OCEAN

ATLANTIC OCEAN

The Bahamas

Cuba

Haiti

Dominican
Republic

Jamaica

Puerto
Rico

Caribbean Sea

COLOMBIA

VENEZUELA

Colombier

Lorient

Anse de
Petit Cul de Sac

GUSTAVIA

Lurin

St. Barthélemy

0   5 mi

0   5 km

Anguilla's Best Beaches

the island's most posh resorts, which is located along the shore.

SANDY GROUND

If your top priority for a beach is buzzy nightlife, head to Sandy Ground. Located on the Northwest coast, it's where everyone seems to end up in Anguilla, especially for parties that spring up often.

SHOAL BAY

Possibly the single most photographed of Anguilla's beaches, Shoal Bay has powder-fine slightly pinkish sand, near-constant light tradewinds, that only-in-the-Caribbean turquoise water, and the spectrum of services that spells the difference between a perfect beach and one that's perfectly extraordinary.

MEADS BAY

Gorgeous Meads Bay stands out because of its top resorts and fine restaurants. Stay at dreamy places like Malliouhana and Carimar Beach Club.

ISLAND HARBOUR

Located on Northeast Anguilla, Island Harbour is

primarily a fishing village but there's a tranquil little beach, too. There are laid-back beach restaurants, and it's a great place to meet locals.

MAUNDAYS BAY

This scenic crescent-shaped beach is known mostly as the home of Belmond Cap Juluca, one of

COVE BAY

Located in the Southwest portion of Anguilla near Rendezvous Bay and Maundays Bay, Cove Bay (like its neighbor beaches) faces St. Maarten and has powdery white sand. One of Anguilla's larger beaches, Cove Bay is great for activities and is a good choice for swimmers, kitesurfers, and folks on horseback.

Cove Bay

larger beaches, Cove Bay is great for activities and is a good choice for swimmers, kitesurfers, and folks on horseback.

RENDEZVOUS BAY
With its dazzling blue water, Rendezvous Bay is a fitting home of the beautiful CuisinArt Golf Resort and Spa as well as Bankie Banx's famous beach bar, the Dune Preserve. It's a long-time favorite of many island visitors because of its striking beauty and pristine sand.

CAPTAIN'S BAY
Although you may have heard of Captain's Bay,

chances are you haven't gone there. Located near the somewhat distant East End of Anguilla, Captain's Bay is not easy to get to: you need to know exactly where you're going (an experienced local guide can help). While there are no signs and no services, you're rewarded with beauty and privacy.

LITTLE BAY
This gray-sand beach is often referred to as "Little Anguilla Beach at Little Bay" and yes, it's quite little. It's also quiet, ultra-relaxing, and only plays host to a few beachgoers at any

given time. And, if you like snorkeling, night dives, or climbing rocks and jumping off the top into the water, this is the spot. You must get here either by climbing down a rock ledge using ropes or by boat from Crocus Bay.

SANDY ISLAND
Sandy Island—a little offshore cay— makes Anguilla seem boisterous by comparison. You must get here by ferry from Sandy Ground, but the trip is worth it: the small but gorgeous bit of beach delivers the true definition of serenity.

Best Restaurants in St. Maarten/St. Martin

LA PATRONA
St. Maarten's one truly authentic Mexican restaurant, La Patrona is on the water's edge at the Dutch side's Simpson Bay Resort. You can dine in the beautiful air-conditioned restaurant or outside on their large seaside patio.

MARIO BISTRO
Located in the Mediterranean-style village of Porto Cupecoy, Mario's eclectic French menu items with a strong Caribbean influence have been delighting visitors for more than 25 years. Whether you seek fine aged beef or the freshest of seafood, don't forget that you must, somehow, leave room for dessert.

IZI RISTORANTE ITALIANO
This upbeat Simpson Bay restaurant is nonstop fun on the surface, but the chef is all business in the kitchen. His insistence on top-notch ingredients has paid off in loyal clients and lots of awards, including best Italian restaurant. Try the tasting menu with outstanding wines, by reservation only.

LA CIGALE
The views of the lagoon from this upscale French restaurant near Marigot are almost as wonderful as the dining experience. From the excellent service to the artistic dish presentation, you'll savor this one well after your vacation is over.

VESNA TAVERNA
Located in Simpson Bay, Vesna's Greek-French fusion restaurant is always a favorite. The owners scour the world for new recipes for their evening specials menu. The restaurant has full American breakfasts (try the bagel tower with lox and egg on their homemade bagels), lunches, or dinner, but the best time to come is Saturday for Greek Night.

SPIGA
At this Italian restaurant, quality ingredients are sourced from around the world, and the result is one of the most spectacular menus in the Caribbean. Located in a beautifully restored old Creole home at the northern end of

Vesna Taverna

Grand Case opposite Tijon Parfumerie, Spiga is open daily except Sunday.

SKIPJACK'S

This big, busy, classic Simpson Bay seafood restaurant has repeatedly been voted the best on the island. Reserve a table on the water for great views of megayachts at the nearby Isle de Sol Marina. SkipJack's sells spiny Caribbean lobster from nearby Saba, cooked several different ways: you'll have to decide if it's more flavorful than New England cold-water lobster, as many claim.

BACCHUS

With a wine cellar that could put those in mainland France to shame, always-busy Bacchus offers a stunning array of fresh French breads, pastries, and deli items. The restaurant is located in the Hope Estate area in Grand Case.

Best Luxury Shops in St. Barth

KALINAS PERLES

Tahitian black pearls and rare fiery pink conch pearls are among the unique finds at this shop, in addition to one-of-a-kind shells and precious stones. *Rue du Général De Gaulle, Gustavia.*

VICTOIRE

Exclusivity is the watchword here. Open only from Thanksgiving through April, the boutique has a Nantucket and Greenwich meets the Caribbean vibe. The company only uses fine fabrics and perfect cuts, so we have to agree when they claim, "You'll never find anywhere else what you'll find here." *Rue du Général de Gaulle, Gustavia.*

KOKON

Peruse a beautifully edited mix of designs, including accessories, shoes, and beach footwear plus designer items from the likes of Birger et Mikkelsen, Mathilde à la Plage, Clovis, bless you by Meli, and others. And shoes? Mais oui, from Heidi Klum. *Rue Fahlberg, at the head of Gustavia harbor.*

ILÉNA

A shop of gorgeous things for gorgeous people, Iléna has incredible beach-wear and lingerie by Chantal Thomas, Andres Sarda, Raffaela D'Angelo, including Swarovski crystal-encrusted bikinis and seashell-encrusted bathing suits. *Villa Creole, St. Jean.*

HERMÈS

The Hermès family's creation of leather and textiles began almost 200 years ago. Hermès in St. Barth today is an independently owned franchise of the legendary business, selling leathers, silk, fragrances, footwear, clothing, and accessories. Prices are slightly less than in the U.S. *Le Carré d'Or, Gustavia.*

MADEMOISELLE HORTENSE

Charming tops and dresses are fashioned out of prints made on the island. The clothing, jewelry, bathing attire, accessories, and exquisite leather goods fills the store with a spectrum of colors. *Rue de la République, Gustavia.*

Kalinas Perles

MARINA ST. BARTH
This trendy resort-wear boutique includes lines sourced from around the world and one created by Marina herself. Lines have included Ondade and Façonnable, and there are high-fashion T-shirts by Eleven Paris and elegant silk tunics by Jodé. *Rue du Roi Oscar II, Gustavia.*

FRENCH INDIES DESIGN
This home furnishing shop on the far side of Gustavia Harbor is the brainchild of Karine Bruneel, a St. Barth-based architect and interior designer. There are lovely items to accent your home, yacht, or restaurant, including furniture, textiles, glassware, and unusual baskets, candles, and pottery. *Rive Gauche, Brigantin mansion, Gustavia.*

How to Decide Between St. Maarten and St. Martin

The Caribbean is full of bucket-list destinations, which makes trying to narrow your next trip down to just one feel impossible. Luckily, St. Martin and St. Maarten allow you to hit two birds with one island. The small 37-square-mile island is split in two. Legend has it that long ago, a Frenchman and Dutchmen raced along the coast in opposite directions. When they met, the governments of France and the Netherlands split the island on that line down the middle. Today, that means visitors get treated to a unique experience: two nationalities, two different vibes—one unbeatable vacation.

Although the gateless border makes it easy to cross from one side to the other, you'll ultimately have to choose where you want to stay: the quieter, culinarily captivating French St. Martin, or the bustling Dutch St. Maarten. Let's be clear, the island is fantastic. You can't make a wrong choice when picking which side to stay on—but you can pick the side that's better for you.

FOR NATURAL BEACHES
St. Martin

There's no shortage of luxuriously catered beaches across the island. You have your pick of sandy shores where you can plop down in an umbrella-shaded lounge chair and have a Caribe in your hand in five minutes. But if you're looking for something a little more secluded, a little more off the beaten track, start your search on the French side. There, you'll find hidden beaches like Happy Bay. Fifteen minutes of walking along a narrow, slightly hilly path (avoiding an occasional cow pie or two) and you'll find yourself in a gorgeous half-moon bay, with just a few other families or seminude sunbathers sharing the palm trees' shade.

INSIDER TIP: Pack a lunch or be prepared to make the short trek back to the beach bars at Friar's Bay for a midday snack—there aren't any facilities at Happy.

FOR HURRICANE RECOVERY
St. Maarten

Walk through any town in St. Maarten and you'll hear a new sound mingled in with the crashing waves of the ocean: the clank of construction equipment. After hurricanes Irma and Maria devastated the island in 2017, the Friendly Island is nearly back to its pre-storm capacity, but it's undeniable that the Dutch side is recovering faster than the French. (There are mutterings on the island that the French government holds some of the blame, with locals saying it's been reluctant to disperse aid money and slow to grant permits to rebuild waterfront shops and restaurants that were destroyed.)

The island will be ready to welcome you, no matter which side you stay on. But if you're at all concerned, stay in St. Maarten, where every other day another old-favorite restaurant reopens its doors.

FOR WORLD-CLASS SHOPPING
St. Maarten

On an island renowned for its (duty-free) jewelry shopping, Philipsburg's Front Street really shines above the rest. The Dutch capital is home to a number of high-class jewelry stores, as well as a charming boardwalk. When cruises are in port, the shopping areas can get crowded—all the more reason to lodge somewhere close by and pop in at your convenience!

INSIDER TIP: For more eclectic boutique-style jewelry, check out Marigot's semiweekly morning markets on the French side.

FOR FOODIES
St. Martin

There's an adage that repeat visitors to the Dutch side use to sum up their decision: Stay on the Dutch side; eat on the French. That's all well and good, but why stay farther from the food than you need to? Stay on the French side and have beach-picnic brunches of fresh-baked baguettes and cheese, afternoon treats of Parisian-quality tarts, and the most sumptuous French Caribbean seafood for dinner. Book a room in Grand Case, the island's culinary capital, and make reservations one night at Bistrot Caraïbes, then wander into one of the tiny Creole eateries called lolos the next.

FOR NUDE BEACHES
St. Martin

Is there anything more French than nude sunbathing? Okay, perhaps cheese, wine, and sex appeal. But part of that last one comes from the suave self-confidence that seems innate to the French—and what could be more self-confident than baring it all? Many beaches on the French side of the island welcome nude sunbathers; some, like the ever-popular Baie Orientale, offer great happy hours if you need an extra shot of confidence to join them.

FOR BOATING CULTURE
St. Maarten

The annual Heineken Regatta in the Port de Plaisance and Simpson Bay area brings crews of enthusiastic amateurs, charters, and serious sailors alike to the largest warm-water regatta in the world. It's hard to tell what the bigger draw is: the races or revelry that follows, with DJs spinning into the early hours of morning for locals and the thousands of visitors that arrive on the island each March. Any other time of the year, Simpson Bay is still a sailor's delight. The Dutch harbor is home to more than a few luxury yachts, and the St. Maarten Yacht Club organizes social and competitive sailing year-round.

INSIDER TIP: Some of us have the means to enjoy a day—or even an entire vacation—on a yacht. For the rest of us, there's the Soggy Dollar and other Simpson Bay bars that open up onto the marina. Gaze on the nautical opulence while sipping a (much more afforda-ble) cocktail.

FOR THE BEST DIVING
St. Maarten

There are plenty of chances to go scuba diving off the Friendly Island's shores. And while it's hard to have a bad dive in the Caribbean, the sites in St. Martin or St. Maarten don't hold a candle to some of the region's best dive spots. Nearby Saba, on the other hand! The dormant volcanic island, visible from St. Maarten's Sunset Beach on clear days, offers some of the best hidden gems for diving in the Caribbean. Ferries leave almost daily for Saba from Philipsburg or Simp-son Bay, but the incomparably shorter and less nauseating flights departing from Princess Juliana International Airport are probably a better bet—even if the landing's a bit nerve-wracking!

FOR BOHO-CHIC CULTURE
St. Martin

The Dutch side's almost overdeveloped infrastructure is admittedly convenient, but it also leaves some travelers feeling like that's all there is, right up until you get to the beach's edge. St. Martin's vibe, on the other hand, is half-boho, half-chic southern France. Think villas nestled into shady hills, colorful little rues in Marigot, and cafés with pastries so good you'll eat them even on a vacation where you spend 80 percent of your day in a swimsuit. On Tuesdays, check out Harmony Night in Grand Case, a festival that's equal parts open-air market and street party, with drink vendors, silversmith artisans, and crêpe-makers selling their wares as a Carnival-esque parade dances past.

FOR THE BEST TIME
St. Martin/St. Maarten

Whatever you do, don't stress about where you stay. American visitors might feel slightly more at home on the Dutch side, where the dollar is the default currency and English is the lingua franca, but you'll find that many vendors on the French half also speak English and will offer you a competitive dollar-to-euro exchange rate. And commitment-phobes need not worry: Crossing from one side to the other is just a matter of minutes, depending on where you are. Sleep at the little beachfront hotel nestled into the cove at Anse Marcel, then hop in your rental car for a day trip to Sunset Beach to marvel at the airport's infamously low landings. No matter which side you choose, you're making a good choice.

Family Travel

All three islands have plenty of activities and attractions that will keep children of all ages (and their parents) busy and interested. Children are generally welcome at restaurants, especially earlier in the evenings.

ST. MAARTEN/ ST. MARTIN

Le Petit Hotel, a boutique property in Grand Case, has full apartment units and a caring management team. Don't miss the ziplines at **Loterie Farm, Rainforest Adventures, or Pelican Peak** ride the **Carousel,** try kiteboarding on **Orient Beach,** and enjoy incredible water sports all over the island. **Pineapple Pete's** suits for easy meals all day long, or try the jerk chicken and salads at **Blue Bitch Bar** in Philipsburg. Vegetarians flock to **Top Carrot.**

ST. BARTH

Children are welcome at most resorts. **Hotel Le Village St. Jean** makes it an easy to walk to beaches or shopping. Only in St. Barth would you find a **Yellow Submarine** from which to observe undersea life in air-conditioned comfort, though quarters are tight for adults. Don't leave without a visit to the **Inter Oceans (Shell) Museum.** Casual dining options include Gustavia's **La Crêperie,** and the loads of local-style grills and pizzerias for take-out.

ANGUILLA

CuisinArt Golf Resort and Spa offers children's programs, babysitting, and a great beach. Many activities are included at **Cap Juluca,** and **Four Seasons** has programs for little kids and a media room and club for teens.

Family dining options include **Blanchard's Beach Shack** and **Picante.** Don't miss a family excursion to gorgeous **Scilly Cay;** wave from the dock and a boat will take you out to the island for a day of snorkeling and fresh grilled fish and lobster. Even nonswimmers can enjoy an excursion on **Junior's Glass Bottom Boat.**

Chapter 2

TRAVEL SMART

Updated by
Jeff Berger

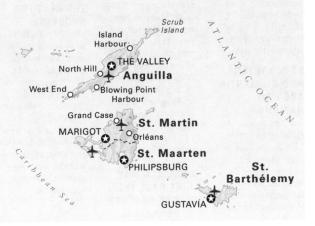

What to Know Before You Go

Which island is best for me? Can I get by with English? When should I go? You may have a few questions before your vacation to the Caribbean islands of St. Maarten/St. Martin, St. Barth & Anguilla. Here's what you need to know before you embark on your next sunny holiday to this tropical paradise so your next sunny holiday runs smoothly.

YOU'LL PROBABLY GO THROUGH ST. MAARTEN FIRST

These islands are close in proximity and connected by frequent ferries and flights. Most travelers, regardless of which island they plan to visit, land in St. Maarten/St. Martin and make their way to their final destination.

ST. MAARTEN AND ST. MARTIN ARE TWO NATIONS

No, it's not a spelling variation. This single island is governed by two countries, St. Maarten by the Netherlands and St. Martin by France.

SOME ISLANDS ARE EASIER TO REACH THAN OTHERS

The hassle factor is low for St. Maarten, and medium to high for Anguilla or St. Barth. Only Princess Juliana International Airport (SXM) in St. Maarten has nonstop flights from the U.S. But you can get a small plane or ferry to Anguilla (AXA) or St. Barth (SBH) from St. Maarten; there are also connecting flights to Anguilla and St. Barth through San Juan.

ANGUILLA MAY JUST HAVE THE NICEST BEACHES

All three islands have beautiful beaches, but those on Anguilla are probably the best.

Baie Orientale on St. Martin is one of the Caribbean's most beautiful beaches, but it's very busy. St. Barth has a wide range of lovely small beaches.

ST. MAARTEN/ST. MARTIN IS THE "FOODIE" ISLAND

While each island has amazing restaurants, St. Maarten and St. Martin stand out. The island has the most restaurants to choose from, and Grand Case in St. Martin, in particular, is renowned for being home to "restaurant row." St. Barth also attracts chefs from around the world.

ST. BARTH IS THE BEST FOR SHOPPING

Yes, St. Maarten has great duty-free shopping, but the posh island of St. Barth is known for having the most high-end boutiques, especially in Gustavia. If you're looking for designer clothing, or simply want to window-shop, St. Barth is your island.

ENGLISH IS WIDELY UNDERSTOOD

Most people involved in the tourism industry on all three islands understand and speak English; French is spoken in St. Barth and French St. Martin.

DON'T JUST VACATION IN "HIGH SEASON"

A Caribbean vacation is a great way to escape winter in much of the U.S., but this is also "high season"—December 15 through April 15, especially the year-end holiday weeks. But wait! Caribbean weather doesn't change much from month to month, although late summer and early fall are generally more humid. So whenever you're in the mood to escape, don't hesitate. "Low season," which is really most of the year, can be quiet, but with lower prices for accommodations and flights. The only caveat: hurricanes are at their peak in September and October.

HURRICANE RECOVERY IS GOING STRONG

Hurricane Irma destroyed parts of these islands in 2017, especially St. Martin and St. Barth. Thanks to their resilient people, the islands rebounded, but you can expect a few old favorites to be gone or relocated. Many hotels and restaurants took the storm as an opportunity to renovate, and are now back and better than ever.

YOU CAN USE U.S. DOLLARS

U.S. currency is accepted almost everywhere in the islands, although the standard currency in French St. Martin and St. Barth is the euro.

DON'T FORGET THE TAX IN ANGUILLA

There's a $20 departure tax in Anguilla when you depart by ferry; it must be paid in cash.

CORAL REEF–SAFE SUNSCREEN IS A MUST

Coral reefs are dying at an alarming rate, and one of the major contributors is sunscreen, more specifically the chemicals oxybenzone and octinoxate. Luckily, numerous companies like Sun Bum, Blue Lizard, and Thinksport offer reef-safe alternatives. So check those labels before you buy your next bottle.

THE DRINKING AGE IS DIFFERENT THAN IN THE U.S.

Visitors don't have to wait until 21 to drink on these islands. Be aware of the minimum legal drinking ages, especially if you're traveling with teens: 18 in St. Maarten/St. Martin and St. Barth, 16 in Anguilla.

Getting Here

St. Maarten/St. Martin, St. Barthélemy, and Anguilla are part of a cluster of islands in the Lesser Antilles that are fairly close together. In fact, the islands are linked by both frequent ferries and small-plane flights. St. Maarten/St. Martin, which has the only international airport among the three capable of handling large passenger jets, is the international flight hub. Most travelers, regardless of which island they plan to visit, land in St. Maarten/St. Martin and make their way to their final destination.

✈ Air

ST. MAARTEN/ ST. MARTIN

There are nonstop flights from Atlanta (Delta), Boston (Jet-Blue, seasonal), Charlotte (AA), Ft. Lauderdale (JetBlue), Miami (AA), New York–JFK (American, Delta, JetBlue), Newark (United), and Philadelphia (AA). There are also some seasonal nonstop charter flights as well as connections via Panama from U.S. cities served by Panamanian carrier Copa. You can also connect in San Juan on Seaborne Air. Many smaller Caribbean-based airlines, including Air Caraïbes, Anguilla Air Services, Caribbean Airlines, Dutch Antilles Express, and Winair (Windward Islands Airways), offer service from other islands in the Caribbean.

ST. BARTHÉLEMY

There are no direct flights to St. Barth. Most North Americans fly first into St. Maarten's Princess Juliana International Airport, from which the island is 10 minutes by air. Winair, which celebrated its 50th anniversary of service to St. Barth in 2013, has regularly scheduled flights from St. Maarten. Tradewind Aviation has regularly scheduled service from San Juan and also does VIP charters. Anguilla Air Services and St. Barth Commuter have scheduled flights and also do charters. You must reconfirm your return interisland flight, even during off-peak seasons, or you may lose your reservations. *Be certain to leave ample time between your scheduled flight and your connection in St. Maarten*—three hours is the minimum recommended (and be aware that luggage frequently doesn't make the trip; your hotel or villa-rental company may be able to send someone to retrieve it). It's a good idea to pack a change of clothes, required medicines, and a bathing suit in your carry-on—or better yet, pack very light and don't check baggage at all.

ANGUILLA

There are no nonstop flights to Anguilla from the United States. TransAnguilla Airways offers daily flights from Antigua, St. Thomas, and St. Kitts. Windward Islands Airways flies several times a day from St. Maarten (SXM). Anguilla Air Services flies from St. Maarten (SXM) and St. Barth (SBH). LIAT comes in from Antigua, Nevis, St. Kitts, St. Thomas, and Tortola.

⚓ Boat

ST. MAARTEN/ ST. MARTIN

You can take ferries to St. Barth (45–80 minutes; €67–€93 from the Dutch or French side, though you can pay in dollars); to Anguilla (20 minutes; $25 from the French side); and to Saba (one to two hours; $90–$100 from the Dutch side). *Babou One,* a stabilized, air-conditioned boat run by West Indies Ferry Express, offers service between Marigot and Gustavia in only 70 minutes, timed to connect with international flights to and from St. Maarten's Princess Juliana Airport.

ST. BARTHÉLEMY

St. Barth can be reached by sea via ferry service or charter boat. There are three companies that provide passenger ferry service between St. Maarten/St. Martin and St. Barth, so check each provider's timetable to determine the most convenient departure. All service is to and from Quai de la République in Gustavia. Voyager offers round trips for about $100 per person from Marigot. Great Bay Express has several round trips a day from Bobby's Marina in St. Maarten for €55 if reserved in advance, or €60 for same-day departures. Private boat charters are also available, but they are very expensive; Master Ski Pilou is one of the companies that offer the service.

ANGUILLA

Ferries run frequently between Anguilla and St. Martin. Boats leave from Blowing Point on Anguilla approximately every half hour from 7:30 am to 6:15 pm and from Marigot, St. Martin, every 45 minutes from 8 am to 7 pm. You pay a $20 departure tax before boarding ($5 for day-trippers—but be sure to make this clear at the window where you pay), in addition to the $15 one-way fare. Children under two years of age are free, children 2–5 are $10. On very windy days the 20-minute trip can be bouncy. The drive between the Marigot ferry terminal and the airport is vastly improved thanks to a new bridge across Simpson Bay. Transfers by

Getting Here

speedboat to Anguilla are available from a new terminal right at the airport, at a cost of about $75 per person (arranged directly with a company, or through your Anguilla hotel). Private ferry companies listed below run six or more round-trips a day, coinciding with major flights, between Blowing Point and the airport in St. Maarten. On the St. Maarten side they will bring you right to the terminal in a van, or you can just walk across the parking lot. These trips are $35 one way or $60 round-trip (cash only), and usually include departure taxes. There are also private charters available.

A late-night sea shuttle service leaves St. Maarten for Anguilla at 10:30 pm. This sea shuttle meets the daily American Airlines flight from Miami, which arrives at 9:55 pm. It then takes you directly to Blowing Point in Anguilla. The trip costs $85 per person. Another sea shuttle, which departs at 7 pm, also goes from St. Maarten to Anguilla. This connects with JetBlue and InselAir flights originating in San Juan. The cost is $65 per person.

Car

ST. MAARTEN/ ST. MARTIN

It's easy to get around the island by car. Most roads are paved and generally in good condition. However, they can be crowded, especially when the cruise ships are in port; you might experience traffic jams, particularly around Marigot and Philipsburg. Be alert for potholes and speed bumps, as well as the island tradition of stopping in the middle of the road to chat with a friend or yield to someone entering traffic. Few roads are identified by name or number, but most have signs indicating the destination. Driving is on the right. There are gas stations in Simpson Bay near the airport as well as in Cole Bay, and on the French side, in Sandy Ground and Marigot.

Car Rentals: You can book a car at Princess Juliana International Airport, where most major rental companies have booths, but it is often much cheaper to reserve a car in advance from home. A shuttle to the rental-car lot is provided. Rates are among the best in the Caribbean, as little as $20–$35 per day. You can rent a car on the French side, but this rarely makes sense for Americans because of unfavorable exchange rates.

ST. BARTHÉLEMY

Roads are sometimes unmarked, so get a map and look for signs pointing to a destination. These will be nailed to posts at all cross-roads. Roads are narrow and sometimes very steep, but recent work has improved roads all over the island; even so, check the brakes and gears of your rental car before you drive away. ■TIP→ **Take a careful inventory of existing dents and scrapes on your rental vehicle with pictures on your smartphone or digital camera.** Maximum speed on the island is 30 mph (50 kph). Driving is on the right, as in the United States and Europe. Parking is an additional challenge. There are two gas stations on the island, one near the airport and one in Lorient. They aren't open after 5 pm, or on Sunday, but the station near the airport has pumps that accept automated payment by card. Considering the short distances, a full tank of gas should last you most of a week.

Car Rentals: You must have a valid driver's license and be 25 or older to rent, and in high season there may be a three-day minimum. During peak periods, such as Christmas week and February, be sure to arrange for your car rental ahead of time. When you make your hotel reservations, ask if the hotel has its own cars available to rent; some hotels provide 24-hour emergency road service—something most rental companies here don't offer. Expect to pay at least $55 per day. A Mini Cooper convertible makes the most of sunny drives.

ANGUILLA

Although most of the rental cars on-island have the driver's side on the left as in North America, Anguillian roads are like those in the United Kingdom—driving is on the left side of the road. It's easy to get the hang of driving on the left, but the roads can be quite rough, so be cautious and observe the 30 mph (48 kph) speed limit. Roundabouts are probably the biggest driving obstacle for most. As you approach, give way to the vehicle on your right; once you're in, you have the right of way.

Car Rentals: A temporary Anguilla driver's license is required to rent a car—you can get into real trouble if you're caught driving without one. You get it for $20 (good for three months) at any of the car-rental agencies at the time you pick up your car; you'll also need your valid driver's license from home. Rental rates start at about $45–$55 per day, plus insurance.

Getting Here

🛵 Scooter

ST. MAARTEN/
ST. MARTIN

Though traffic can be heavy, speeds are generally slow, so a moped can be a good way to get around. Scooters rent for as low as €25 per day and motorbikes for €37 a day at Eugene Moto, on the French side.

ST. BARTH

Several companies rent motorbikes, scooters, mopeds, and mountain bikes. Motorbikes go for about $30 per day and require a $100 deposit. Helmets are required. Scooter and motorbike rental places are mostly along rue de France in Gustavia and around the airport in St-Jean.

🚕 Taxi

ST. MAARTEN/
ST. MARTIN

There is a government-sponsored taxi dispatcher at the airport and at the harbor. Posted fares are for one or two people. Add $5 for each additional person, $1 to $2 per bag. It costs about $18 from the airport to Philipsburg or Marigot, and about $30 to Dawn Beach. After 10 pm fares go up 25%, and after midnight 50%. Licensed drivers can be identified by the "taxi" license plate on the Dutch side (or some new "T" plates) and the TXI license plate on the French. You can hail cabs on the street or call the taxi dispatch to have one sent for you. Fixed fares apply from Juliana International Airport and the Marigot ferry to the various hotels around the island. There are unlicensed, uninsured cabs on the island without the proper license plates; they're illegal and should be avoided.

ST. BARTHÉLEMY

Taxis are expensive and not particularly easy to arrange, especially in the evening. There's a taxi station at the airport and another in Gustavia; from elsewhere you must contact a dispatcher in Gustavia or St-Jean. Fares are regulated by the Collectivite, and drivers accept both dollars and euros. If you go out to dinner by taxi, let the restaurant know if you will need a taxi at the end of the meal, and they will call one for you.

ANGUILLA

Taxis are fairly expensive, so if you plan to explore the island's many beaches and restaurants, it may be more cost-effective to rent a car. Taxi rates are regulated by the government, and there are fixed fares from point to point, which are listed in brochures the drivers should have handy and are also

published in the local guides.
It's $26 from the airport or $22
from Blowing Point Ferry to
West End hotels. Posted rates
are for one or two people; each
additional passenger adds
$5 to the total, and there is a
$1 charge for each piece of
luggage beyond the allotted
two. You can also hire a taxi for
the hourly rate of about $28.
Surcharges of $4–$10 apply to
trips after 6 pm. You'll always
find taxis at the Blowing Point
Ferry landing and at the airport.
You'll need to call them to pick
you up from hotels and restaurants, and arrange ahead with
the driver who took you if you
need a taxi late at night from
one of the nightclubs or bars.

Before You Go

🌐 Passport

A valid passport and a return or ongoing ticket is required for travel to Anguilla, St. Barthélemy, and St. Maarten/St. Martin. There are no border controls whatsoever between the Dutch and French sides of St. Maarten/St. Martin. Passports must be valid for at least three months from the date of entry to the territory of St. Barthélemy.

🪪 Visa

Visas are NOT required for travelers with a passport issued by the United States to a Caribbean nation. Passport-holders from the Middle East, African nations, most of Asia, and parts of Central and South America must apply for a tourist visa.

✏️ Immunizations

No specific immunizations or vaccinations are required for visits to the Caribbean islands, but children should be up-to-date on their routine immunizations (DTaP, MMR, influenza, chicken pox, and polio).

📅 When to Go

The Caribbean high season runs from about December 15 through April 15—great for escaping winter. The Christmas holiday season is very busy in St. Martin/St. Maarten and an especially expensive time to visit Anguilla and St. Barth, and you may very well pay double during this period, with minimum rental requirements for some villas and hotels. After April prices may be 20% to 50% less, and you can often book on short notice. Some hotels and restaurants close for all or part of September and October.

CLIMATE

The average year-round temperatures for the region are 78°F to 88°F. The temperature extremes are 65°F low, 95°F high; but, as everyone knows, it's the humidity, not the heat, that makes you suffer—especially when the two go hand in hand. The high-season months of December through April generally provide warm, sunny days with little humidity. The off-season months, particularly August through November, are the most humid. As part of the late-fall rainy season, hurricanes occasionally sweep through the Caribbean. Check the news daily and keep abreast of brewing tropical storms. The rainy season consists mostly of brief showers interspersed with sunshine. You can watch the clouds thicken, feel the rain, then have brilliant sunshine dry you off, all while remaining on your lounge chair. A spell of overcast days or heavy rainfall is unusual.

HURRICANE SEASON

The Atlantic hurricane season lasts from June 1 through November 30, but it's fairly rare to see a large storm in either June or November. Most major hurricanes occur between August and October, with the peak season in September. Since 2017's Hurricane Irma, hotels and restaurants have rebuilt stronger and standards have been raised to a much higher level.

If a hurricane warning is issued and flights to your destination are disrupted, virtually every Caribbean resort will waive cancellation and change penalties and allow you to rebook your trip for a later date. Some will allow you to cancel if a hurricane threatens to strike, even if flights aren't canceled. Some will give you a refund if you have prepaid for your stay, while others will expect you to rebook your trip for a later date. Some large resort companies—including Sandals and SuperClubs—have "hurricane guarantees," but they apply only when flights have been canceled or when a hurricane is sure to strike.

If you plan to travel to the Caribbean during the hurricane season, it is wise to buy travel insurance that allows you to cancel for any reason. This kind of coverage can be expensive (up to 10% of the value of the trip); but if you have to prepay far in advance for an expensive vacation package, the peace of mind may be worth it. Just be sure to read the fine print; some policies don't kick in unless flights are canceled and the hurricane strikes, something you may not be assured of until the day you plan to travel. To get a complete cancellation policy, you must usually buy your insurance within a week of booking your trip. If you wait to purchase insurance until after the hurricane warning is issued, it will be too late.

Track those hurricanes. To keep a close eye on the Caribbean during hurricane season, several websites track hurricanes as they progress: ⊕ *www. accuweather.com*, ⊕ *hurricanetrack. com*, ⊕ *www.nhc.noaa.gov*, and ⊕ *www.weather.com*.

Essentials

🛏 Lodging

ST. MAARTEN/ ST. MARTIN

St. Maarten/St. Martin has the widest array of accommodations of any of the three islands, with a range of large resort hotels, small resorts, time-shares, condos, private villas, and small B&Bs scattered across the island. Most of the larger resorts are concentrated in Dutch St. Maarten. Visitors find a wide range of choices in many different price ranges.

ST. BARTHÉLEMY

The vast majority of accommodations on St. Barth are in private villas in a wide variety of levels of luxury and price; villas are often priced in U.S. dollars. The island's small luxury hotels are exceedingly expensive, made more so for Americans because prices are in euros. A few modest and moderately priced hotels do exist on the island, but there's nothing on St. Barth that could be described as cheap, though there are now a few simple guest houses and inns that offer acceptable accommodations for what in St. Barth is a bargain price (not far over €100 per night in low season in some cases).

ANGUILLA

Anguilla has several large luxury resorts, a few smaller resorts and guesthouses, and a rather large mix of private condos and villas. Lodging on Anguilla is generally fairly expensive, but there are a few more modestly priced choices.

🍽 Dining

St. Maarten/St. Martin, Anguilla, and St. Barth are known for their fine restaurants. *For more information on local cuisine and dining possibilities, see the individual island chapters. For information on food-related health issues, see Health below.*

PAYING

Credit cards are widely accepted on all three islands. *For more information, see the individual island chapters.*

➕ Health

There's been a sharp decrease in cases of mosquito-borne illnesses including Dengue Fever, Chikungunya, and Zika across the region thanks to increased vigilance by all three islands' governments in the wake of cases reported in the mid '00s. Still, you should be cautious. Although there are no effective vaccines to prevent them, visitors to the region should protect themselves with mosquito repellent (particularly repellent containing DEET, which has been deemed the most effective) and keep arms and legs covered at sunset, when some mosquitoes may be particularly active.

There are no particular ongoing problems regarding food and water safety in St. Maarten/ St. Martin, Anguilla, or St. Barth. If you have an especially sensitive stomach, you may wish to drink only bottled water; also be sure that food has been thoroughly cooked and is served to you fresh and hot. Peel fruit. If you have problems, mild cases of traveler's diarrhea may respond to Pepto-Bismol. Imodium may be necessary if you have persistent problems. Be sure to drink plenty of fluids; if you can't keep fluids down, seek medical help immediately.

MEDICAL INSURANCE AND ASSISTANCE

Consider buying trip insurance with medical-only coverage. Neither Medicare nor some private insurers cover medical expenses anywhere outside the United States. Medical-only policies typically reimburse you for medical care (excluding that related to pre-existing conditions) and hospitalization abroad. Consider programs

like "SkyMed," which takes Americans and Canadians back to their home-city hospitals instead of "to the nearest approprite facility," which is what most credit-card based medical evacuation insurance plans actually do.

➕ Safety
ST. MAARTEN/ ST. MARTIN

Petty crime can be a problem on both sides of the island, though robberies have been declining for several years. Always lock your valuables and travel documents in your room safe or your hotel's front-desk safe. Don't ever leave anything in the car, even in the trunk or glove compartment. When driving, keep your seatbelt on and the car doors locked. Don't drink and drive; penalties for violating the laws are severe. Never leave anything unattended at the beach. Despite the romantic imagery of the Caribbean, it's not good policy to take long walks along the beach at night. You should be on guard even during the day. Don't flash cash or jewelry, carry your handbag securely and zipped, and park in the busier and better-lit areas of parking lots in towns and at beaches. Other suggestions include carrying only your driver's license

Essentials

and a photocopy of your passport with you for identification, leaving the original in your hotel safe. In general, use the same caution here as you would use at home.

ST. BARTHÉLEMY

There's relatively little crime on St. Barth. Visitors can travel anywhere on the island with confidence. Most hotel rooms have safes for your valuables. As anywhere, don't tempt loss by leaving cameras, laptops, or jewelry out in plain sight in your hotel room or villa or in your car. Don't walk barefoot at night: there are venomous centipedes that can inflict a remarkably painful sting. If you ask residents, they will tell you that they only drink bottled water, although most cook or make coffee with tap water.

ANGUILLA

Anguilla is a quiet, relatively safe island, but crime has been on the rise, and there's no sense in tempting fate by leaving your valuables unattended in your hotel room, on the beach, or in your car. Avoid remote beaches, and lock your car, hotel room, and villa. Most hotel rooms are equipped with a safe for stashing your valuables.

💲 Money

Prices *throughout this guide* are given for adults. Substantially reduced fees are almost always available for children, students, and senior citizens. Refrences to credit cards are made only in those cases where they are not accepted.

ST. MAARTEN/ ST. MARTIN

Legal tender on the Dutch side is the Netherlands Antilles florin (guilder) but almost everyone accepts U.S. dollars. On the French side, the currency is the euro, but most establishments accept dollars. At this writing, quite a few restaurants continue to offer one-to-one euro-for-dollar equivalency for purchases made in cash. ATMs dispense dollars, euros, or guilders, depending on where you are.

ST. BARTHÉLEMY

Legal tender is the euro, but U.S. dollars are widely accepted. ATMs are common and dispense only euros.

ANGUILLA

Legal tender is the Eastern Caribbean (EC) dollar, but U.S. dollars are widely accepted. ATMs dispense both U.S. and EC dollars. *All prices quoted in this chapter are in U.S. dollars.*

Taxes

ST. MAARTEN/ ST. MARTIN
Departure tax from Juliana Airport is $10 to destinations within the Netherlands Antilles and $30 to all other destinations. It is usually included in your air ticket. It will cost you €3 (usually included in the ticket price) to depart by plane from Aéroport de L'Espérance and $5 (the rate can change) by ferry to Anguilla from Marigot's pier. Hotels on the Dutch side add a 15% service charge to the bill as well as a 5% government tax. Hotels on the French side add 10%–15% and generally 5% tax.

ST. BARTHÉLEMY
The island charges a $5 departure tax when your next stop is another French island, $10 to anywhere else payable in cash only (dollars or euros). Some hotels add a 10% service charge. Sometimes it is included in the room rate, so check. There is a 5% room tax on hotels and villa rentals.

ANGUILLA
The departure tax is $20 for adults and $10 for children, payable in cash, at the airport at Blowing Point Ferry Terminal. If you are staying in Anguilla but day-tripping to St. Martin, be sure to mention it, and the rate will be only $5. A 10% accommodations tax is added to hotel bills.

Tipping

ST. MAARTEN/ ST. MARTIN
Service charges may be added to hotel and restaurant bills on the Dutch side (otherwise tip 15%–18%). Check bills carefully so you don't inadvertently tip twice. On the French side, a service charge is customary; on top of the included service it is customary to leave an extra 5%–10% *in cash* for the server. Taxi drivers, porters, and maids depend on tips.

ST. BARTHÉLEMY
Restaurants include a 15% service charge in their published prices, but it's common French practice to leave 5% to 10% more in cash, even if you have paid by credit card. Most taxi drivers don't expect a tip.

ANGUILLA
Despite any service charge, it's usually expected that you will tip more—$5 per day for housekeeping, $20 for a helpful concierge, and $10 per day to beach attendants. Many restaurants include a service charge of 10% to 15% on the bill; if there's no surcharge, tip about 15%. Taxi drivers usually receive 10% of the fare.

Weddings and Honeymoons

There's no question that St. Maarten/St. Martin, St. Barth, and Anguilla are three of the Caribbean's foremost honeymoon destinations. Romance is in the air here, and the white, sandy beaches and turquoise water, swaying palm trees, balmy tropical breezes, and perpetual summer sunshine put people in the mood for love. Destination weddings—no longer exclusive to celebrities and the super rich—are also popular on Anguilla and Dutch St. Maarten, but French residency requirements make getting married in French St. Martin or St. Barth too difficult. All the larger resorts in Anguilla and St. Maarten have wedding planners to help you with the paperwork and details.

THE BIG DAY
Choosing the Perfect Place.
When choosing a location, remember that you really have two choices to make: the ceremony location and where to have the reception, if you're having one. For the former, there are beaches, bluffs overlooking beaches, gardens, private residences, resort lawns, and, of course, places of worship. As for the reception, there are these same choices, as well as restaurants. If you decide to go outdoors, remember the seasons (yes, the Caribbean has seasons). Be sure you have a backup plan in case it rains. If your heart is set on an outdoor wedding at sunset, match the time of your ceremony to the time the sun sets at that time of year.

Finding a Wedding Planner.
If you're planning to invite more than an officiant and your loved one to your wedding ceremony, seriously consider on-island wedding planners who can help with selecting a location, designing the floral decor, and recommending a reliable photographer. They can plan the menu, and suggest local traditions to incorporate into your ceremony. Of course, all the larger resorts have their own wedding planners. If you're planning a resort wedding, work with the on-site wedding coordinator to prepare a detailed list of the exact services they'll provide. If your idea of your wedding doesn't match their services, try a different resort. Or look for an independent wedding planner. Both Anguilla and St. Maarten have independent wedding planners who are not employed by resorts.

Legal Requirements.
There are minimal residency requirements on Anguilla and St. Maarten, and no blood tests or shots are required on either island. On Anguilla, you can get a wedding license in two working days; paperwork in St.

Maarten has to be submitted 14 days in advance, but there is no residency requirement there. You need to supply proof of identity (a passport or certified copy of your birth certificate signed by a notary public, though in Anguilla even a driver's license with a photo will do). You must provide proof of divorce with the original or certified copy of the divorce decree if you are divorced, or copy of the death certificate if you are a widow or widower.

Wedding Attire. In the Caribbean, basically anything goes, from long, formal dresses with trains to white bikinis. Floral sundresses are fine, too. Men can wear tuxedos or a simple pair of solid-color slacks with a nice white linen shirt. If you want formal dress and a tuxedo, it's usually better to bring your formal attire with you.

Photographs. Deciding whether to use the photographer supplied by your resort or an independent photographer is an important choice. Resorts that host a lot of weddings usually have their own photographers, but you can also find independent, professional island-based photographers, and an independent wedding planner will know the best in the area. Look at the portfolio (many photographers now have websites), and decide

whether this person can give you the kind of memories you are looking for. If you're satisfied with the photographer that your resort uses, then make sure you see proofs and order prints before you leave the island. In any case, arrange to take a CD home with you of HD photos, because uploading them via the Internet is a time-consuming frustration what with (typically slow) Caribbean connections.

THE HONEYMOON

Do you want champagne and strawberries delivered to your room each morning? An infinity pool in which to float? A five-star restaurant in which to dine? Then a resort is the way to go, and both Anguilla and St. Maarten have options in different price ranges (though Anguilla resorts are more luxurious and more expensive as a rule). Whether you want a luxurious experience or a more modest one, you'll certainly find someplace romantic to which you can escape. You can usually stay on at the resort where your wedding was held. On the other hand, maybe you want your own private home. In that case, a private vacation-rental home or condo is the answer.

On the Calendar

January

St. Barth Carnival. In St. Barth, celebrations begin in late January and lead up to Mardi Gras in February.

St. Barth Music Festival. Showcasing a wide variety of musical and dance performances, the festival is usually held the second and third weeks of the month. ⊕ *www.stbartsmusicfestival.org*

February

St. Barth Mardi Gras. Carnival celebrations end with a bang on Fat Tuesday.

Moonsplash, Anguilla. Visiting musicians join regional reggae superstar Bankie Banx for this annual music festival. ⊕ *www.whatwedoinanguilla.com*

March

St. Maarten Heineken Regatta. The regatta in early March brings sailors and partygoers from all over the world. As many as 300 sailboats from around the world compete. ⊕ *heinekenregatta.com*

SXM Music Festival. This five-day music festival in St. Martin features a line up of electronic and house musicians.

April

Festival del Mar, Anguilla. Celebrate Anguilla culture during this Easter weekend festival at Island Harbour. ⊕ *www.whatwedoinanguilla.com*

Les Voiles de Saint Barth. An international regatta draws crowds.

St. Maarten Carnival. The big event follows Easter with parades, great food, and music for all.

St. Barth Festival of Caribbean Cinema. Celebrate Caribbean-made documentaries and feature films. ⊕ *www.stbarthff.org*

May

Anguilla Day. Mark your calendar for May 30, when there is a round-the-island race.

Anguilla Regatta. The national love for boat racing peaks at this event. ⊕ *www.anguilla-regatta.com*

July

Bastille Day. St. Barth and St. Martin both celebrate this French holiday of the storming of the Bastille, which kicked off the French Revolution, with fireworks.

August

Boat Races, Anguilla. The races start the first Monday in August, with 10 days of beauty pageants, nonstop partying, and the races themselves in old-fashioned wooden boats. The "landracers" following onshore have as much fun as the boats.

St. Barth Summer Sessions. This event features 30 top musicians from around the world over 10 days. ⊕ *www.french-caribbean.com/st-barthelemy*

Shopping Festival, St. Barth. Browse the high-end boutiques here during the first two weeks of August.

November

Culinary Month, St. Maarten. A month of events makes this foodie destination paradise.

December

New Year's Eve, St. Barth. Locals join visiting boats for a round-the-island regatta, and a fantastic fireworks display over Gustavia Harbor.

Great Itineraries

Here are some suggestions for how to make the most of your trip to the islands, whichever one you choose.

A PERFECT DAY IN ST. MAARTEN/ST. MARTIN

On the French side (St. Martin)? In the morning head to Loterie Farm on the slopes of Pic Paradis to take advantage of the hiking trails or try the zipline, a favorite activity for families. You can stay and have lunch in the café, and lounge around the beautiful spring-fed swimming pool. If you are hot, head right to Baie Orientale, where you can rent some chairs and umbrellas from one of the beach clubs and take advantage of the lovely surf. If you get hungry, you can have snacks or lunch there, too. In the late afternoon, a nap is in order, but you have to be awake before sunset. For a splurge, have your sunset cocktail at the bar of La Samanna before heading to one of the restaurants in Grand Case like La Cigale for a perfect dinner. Try the Calmos Café to get the party started.

If you're on the Dutch side, St. Maarten, try the zipline in Philipsburg for views high above the bustling town, or choose a beach for a more relaxed morning. Cupecoy and Simpson Bay are both top-notch, and Maho Beach is a top choice for watching planes fly low overhead. The afternoon is a good time to stroll along Front Street in Philipsburg, because you can duck into one of the many air-conditioned stores to escape the heat (and take advantage of duty-free shopping). For dinner, head to Izi Ristorante Italiano in Simpson Bay and cap off the night with a drink at Karakter Beach Lounge or Ocean Lounge.

A PERFECT DAY IN ST. BARTH

Have your café au lait and croissant in a harborside café in Gustavia, and explore some of the many boutiques on Quai de la République. If you tire of the hubbub, have lunch in quieter St-Jean and then shop and stroll some more. If you're not a shopper, tie on your sneakers and hike for half an hour down the path to the secluded cove at Colombier, take a snorkeling excursion, or go deep-sea fishing. Be sure to get a late-afternoon nap, because the nightlife in St. Barth doesn't get going until late. After a sunset cocktail in Gustavia, have dinner at one of the island's many great restaurants. Perhaps you'll choose Le Toiny, with its excellent views, or Le Ti St. Barth Caribbean Tavern, which is as much a gathering spot as a restaurant. By the time dessert comes, someone is sure to be dancing on the tables.

Late-night partying really gets going after midnight.

A PERFECT DAY IN ANGUILLA

The perfect day in Anguilla often involves the least activity. After breakfast, head to powdery Shoal Bay. If you get tired of sunning and dozing, take a ride on Junior's Glass Bottom Boat, or arrange a wreck dive at Shoal Bay Scuba. Have lunch at one of the beachside restaurants and relax a little more. In the late afternoon, head back to your hotel room to shower and change before going to Elvis' Beach Bar to watch the sunset with a cold rum punch. Have dinner at one of the island's great restaurants.

Contacts

Air

AIRPORTS

Aéroport de L'Espérance (SFG). ✉ *Rte. de l'Espérance, Grand Case* ☎ *0590/27–11–00* ⊕ *www.saintmartin-airport. com.* **Clayton J. Lloyd International Airport.** ☎ *264/498–4141* ⊕ *www.gov.ai/airport.php.* **Gustaf III Airport (SBH).** ✉ *St. Jean Rd., St-Jean* ☎ *0590/27–75–81.* **Princess Juliana International "SXM" Airport (SXM).** ☎ *721/546–7542* ⊕ *www. sxmairport.com.*

AIRLINE CONTACTS

Air Caraïbes. ☎ *0590/52–05–10* ⊕ *www.aircaraibes.com.* **American Airlines.** ☎ *721/545–2040 Local SXM number for reservations, 800/433–7300 AA's main number* ⊕ *www.aa.com.* **Caribbean Airlines.** ☎ *721/546–7610* ⊕ *www.caribbean-airlines.com.* **Delta Airlines.** ☎ *721/546–7615, 800/221–1212* ⊕ *www.delta. com.* **JetBlue.** ☎ *721/546–7797, 877/306–4939* ⊕ *www. jetblue.com.* **St. Barth Commuter.** ☎ *0590/27–54–54* ⊕ *www. stbarthcommuter.com.* **United Airlines.** ☎ *800/864–8331* ⊕ *www.united.com.* **Winair.** ☎ *721/545–4237* ⊕ *www.fly-winair.sx.*

LOCAL AIRLINE CONTACTS

Anguilla Air Services. ☎ *264/498–5922* ⊕ *www. anguillaairservices.com.*

Trans Anguilla Airways. ☎ *264/498–5922* ⊕ *www. transanguilla.com.* **St. Barth Commuter.** ☎ *0590/27–54–54* ⊕ *www.stbarthcommuter.com.* **Tradewind Aviation.** ☎ *203/267–3305* ⊕ *www.flytradewind. com.* **Winair.** ☎ *0590/27–61–01, 866/466–0410* ⊕ *www.fly-winair.com.*

🚗 Car

CAR-RENTAL CONTACTS

Avis. ✉ *Airport Rd., Simpson Bay* ☎ *721/545–2847, 800/331–1084* ⊕ *www.avis-sxm.com.* **Dollar/Thrifty Car Rental.** ✉ *102 Airport Rd.* ☎ *721/545–2393* ⊕ *www.dollarthriftysxm.com.* **Empress Rent-a-Car.** ☎ *721/545–2062* ⊕ *www.empressrentacar. com.* **Golfe Car Rental.** ✉ *Rte. de l'Espérance, Grand Case* ☎ *0690/35–04–75* ⊕ *www. golfecarrental.com.* **Hertz.** ✉ *82 Airport Rd., Simpson Bay* ☎ *721/545–4541* ⊕ *www.hertz. sxmrentacar.com.* **Unity Car Rental.** ✉ *6 Sister Modesta Rd., Simpson Bay* ☎ *721/520–5767* ⊕ *www.unitycarrental.com.* **Leisure Car Rental St. Maarten.** ✉ *Leisure Car Rental, 130 Airport Rd.* ✛ *About 1/5 mile east of the Princess Juliana Terminal* ☎ *721/581–8577* ⊕ *www. leisurecarrentalsxm.com.* **Turbé.** ☎ *0590/27–71–42* ⊕ *www. turbe-car-rental.com.* **Gumbs.** ☎ *0590/27–75–32* ⊕ *www.*

gumbs-car-rental.com. **Andy's Car Rental.** ☎ 264/584–7010 ⊕ www.andyrentals.com. **Bryans Car Rental.** ☎ 264/497–6407 ⊕ www.bryanscarrentals. com. **Triple K Car Rental/Hertz.** ✉ Airport Rd. ☎ 264/497–2934 ⊕ www.hertz.com. **Barthloc Rental.** ✉ Rue de France, Gustavia ☎ 0590/27–52–81 ⊕ www.barthloc.com. **Chez Béranger.** ✉ 21 rue du général de Gaulle, Gustavia ☎ 0590/27–89–00 ⊕ www.beranger-rental. com.

🚢 Ferry

ST. MAARTEN/ST. MARTIN FERRIES

Saba Ferries. ☎ 599/416–2299 ⊕ www.sabaferry.com. **Aqua Mania Adventures.** ✉ Simpson Bay Resort Marina Plaza, Simpson Bay ☎ 721/544–2640 ⊕ www.stmaarten-activities. com. **Great Bay Express.** ✉ Bobby's Marina Village, Philipsburg ☎ 721/542–0032 Dutch side, 690/88–38–99 French side ⊕ www.greatbayferry.com. **Link Ferries.** ☎ 264/772–6208 ⊕ www.link.ai. **Voyager.** ☎ 0590/87–10–68 ⊕ www. voy12.com.

ST. BARTHÉLEMY BOAT AND FERRY CONTACTS

Great Bay Express. ✉ Quai Gustavia, Gustavia ☎ 721/520–5015 ⊕ www.greatbayferry. com. **Master Ski Pilou.**

☎ 0590/27–91–79 ⊕ www. masterski-pilou.com. **Voyager.** ☎ 0590/87–10–68 ⊕ www. voy12.com.

ANGUILLA CONTACTS

Funtime Ferry. ☎ 866/978–8529 ⊕ www.funtimecharters.com. **GB Ferries.** ☎ 264/235–6205, 321/406–0414 in U.S. ⊕ www. gbferries.com. **Link Ferries.** ☎ 264/772–4901 ⊕ www. linkferry.com.

🚕 Taxi

Dutch St. Maarten Taxi Association. ☎ 721/543–7814, 721/543–7815 ⊕ www.taxist-maarten.com. **Juliana Airport Taxi Dispatch.** ☎ 721/542–1680 ⊕ www.sxmairporttaxis. com. **Taxis.** ☎ 0590/52–40–40, 0590/27–75–81. **Blowing Point Ferry Taxi Stand.** ☎ 264/497–6089 ⊕ caribya.com/anguilla/ taxis. **Taxi Prestige.** ☎ 0590/27–70–57. **Maurice & Sons Exquisite Taxi Services.** ☎ 264/235–2676 ⊕ www.msexquisiteshuttle. com.

➕ Health and Safety

EMERGENCY SERVICES

Dutch-side emergencies. ☎ 911, 721/542–2222 most reliable in emergencies. **French-side emergencies.** ☎ 17, 590/52–25–52.

Contacts

📍 Visitor Information

Dutch-side Tourist Information Bureau. ☎ *721/542–2337* ⊕ *www.vacationstmaarten. com.* **French-side Office de Tourisme.** ✉ *Rte. de Sandy Ground, Marigot* ☎ *0590/87–57–21* ⊕ *www.st-martin.org.* **Office du Tourisme.** ✉ *Quai Général de Gaulle, Gustavia* ☎ *0590/27–87–27* ⊕ *www.saintbarth-tourisme.com.* **Anguilla Tourist Board.** ✉ *Coronation Ave., The Valley* ☎ *264/497–2759* ⊕ *www.ivisitanguilla.com.*

Chapter 3

ST. MAARTEN/
ST. MARTIN

Updated by
Jeff Berger

⊙ Sights   🍴 Restaurants   🏨 Hotels   🛍 Shopping   🍸 Nightlife
★★★★★   ★★★★★   ★★★★☆   ★★★★★   ★★★★★

WELCOME TO ST. MAARTEN/ST. MARTIN

TOP REASONS TO GO

★ **Great Food:** The island has so many good places to dine that you could eat out for a month (or six) and never repeat a restaurant visit.

★ **Lots of Shops:** Philipsburg is one of the top shopping spots in the Caribbean and the galleries and boutiques of Marigot and Grand Case bring a touch of France.

★ **Beaches Large and Small:** Thirty-seven picture-perfect beaches are spread out across the island; some are clothing-optional.

★ **Sports Galore:** The wide range of land and water sports adventures will satisfy almost any need and give you the perfect excuse to try everything from ATVs to ziplines.

★ **Variety of Nightlife:** After-dark entertainment options include shows, lounges, discos, beach bars, and casinos.

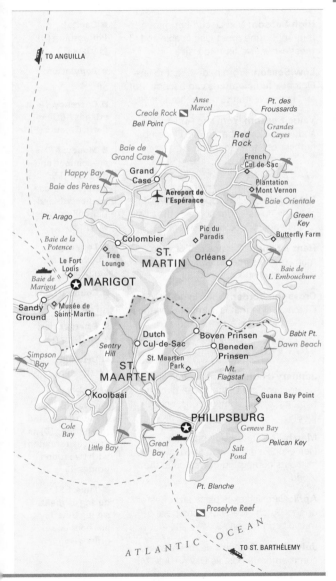

TO ANGUILLA

Creole Rock
Bell Point

Anse Marcel

Pt. des Froussards

Grandes Cayes

Red Rock

Baie de Grand Case

French Cul de Sac

Happy Bay

Baie des Pères

Grand Case

Aeroport de l'Espérance

Plantation Mont Vernon

Baie Orientale

Pt. Arago

Baie de la Potence

Colombier

Pic du Paradis

Green Key

Butterfly Farm

ST. MARTIN

Tree Lounge

Orléans

Le Fort Louis

MARIGOT

Baie de Marigot

Baie de L'Embouchure

Sandy Ground

Musée de Saint-Martin

Simpson Bay

Sentry Hill

Dutch Cul-de-Sac

Boven Prinsen

Beneden Prinsen

Babit Pt.

Dawn Beach

St. Maarten Park

ST. MAARTEN

Mt. Flagstaf

Koolbaai

Guana Bay Point

Cole Bay

PHILIPSBURG

Geneve Bay

Pelican Key

Little Bay

Great Bay

Salt Pond

Pt. Blanche

Proselyte Reef

ATLANTIC OCEAN

TO ST. BARTHÉLEMY

ISLAND SNAPSHOT

WHEN TO GO

High Season: Mid-December through mid-April is the most fashionable and most expensive time to visit.

Low Season: From mid-August to late October, temperatures can become hot and humid, with the risk of hurricanes.

Value Season: From late April to July and again November to mid-December, hotel prices tend to drop.

WAYS TO SAVE

Eat at *lolos*. SXM's' open-air roadside grills, or "lolos," offer some of the best and cheapest food on the island.

Rent a condo. Condos can provide many of the same amenities as pricey villas, including kitchens.

Cross the border. When in doubt, go Dutch ... side that is. Almost everything is cheaper there.

BIG EVENTS

January–February: The French side's Carnival is a pre-Lenten bash of costume parades, music competitions, and feasts.

March: The Dutch side hosts the Heineken Regatta, with as many as 200 sailboats competing from around the world.

April: Carnival takes place after Easter on the Dutch side with a parade and music competition.

July: On the French side, celebrations commemorate Bastille Day on July 14.

AT A GLANCE

■ **Capital:** Phillipsburg (D); Marigot (F)

■ **Population:** 77,740

■ **Currency:** Netherlands Antilles florin (D); euro (F)

■ **Money:** ATMs are common and dispense U.S. dollars or euros; credit cards and U.S. dollars widely accepted.

■ **Language:** Dutch, French, English

■ **Country Code:** ☎ 1 721 (D); 1 590 (F)

■ **Emergencies:** ☎ 911 (D); 17 (F)

■ **Driving:** On the right

■ **Electricity:** Plugs are U.S. standard two- and three-prong (D) and European standard with two round prongs (F)

■ **Time:** EST during daylight saving time; one hour ahead otherwise

St. Maarten/St. Martin is unique among Caribbean destinations. The 37-square-mile (96-square-km) island is a seamless place (there are no border gates), but it is governed by two nations—the Netherlands and France—and has residents from more than 100 countries. A call from the Dutch side to the French is an international call, currencies are different, electric current differs, and even the vibe is different. Only the island of Hispaniola, which encompasses Haiti and the Dominican Republic, is in a similar position in the Caribbean.

Happily for Americans, who make up the majority of visitors to St. Maarten/St. Martin, English works in both nations. Dutch St. Maarten might feel particularly comfortable for Americans: the prices are a bit lower (not to mention in U.S. dollars), the big hotels have casinos, and there is more nightlife. Huge cruise ships disgorge masses of shoppers into the Philipsburg shopping area at midmorning, when roads may become congested. But once you pass the meandering, unmarked border to the French side, you find a hint of the south of France: quiet countryside, fine cuisine, and in Marigot, a walkable harbor area with outdoor cafés, a great outdoor market, and some shops to explore.

Almost 4,000 years ago, it was salt and not tourism that drove this little island's economy. Arawak Indians, the island's first known inhabitants, prospered until the warring Caribs invaded, adding the peaceful Arawaks to their list of conquests. Columbus spotted the isle on November 11, 1493, and named it after St. Martin (whose feast day is November 11), but it wasn't populated by Europeans until the 17th century, when it was claimed by the Dutch, French, and Spanish. The Dutch and French finally joined forces to claim the island in 1644, and the Treaty of Concordia partitioned the territory in 1648. According to legend the border was drawn along the line where a French man and a Dutch man, walking from opposite coasts, met.

Both sides of the island offer a touch of European culture along with a lot of laid-back Caribbean ambience. Water sports both serene and extreme abound—diving, snorkeling, sailing, wind-surfing, kitesurfing, ziplining, and even hover-boarding. With soft trade winds cooling the subtropical climate, it's easy to while away the day relaxing on one of the 37 beaches, strolling Philipsburg's boardwalk, shopping along Philipsburg's Front Street or the harbors of Marigot. Although luck is an important commodity at St. Maarten's dozen or so casinos, chance plays no part in finding a good meal at the hundreds of excellent restaurants or after-dark fun in the subtle to sizzling nightlife.

Planning

Getting Here and Around

AIR TRAVEL

More than 20 carriers fly to the island. There are nonstop flights from Atlanta (Delta, seasonal), Boston (JetBlue, seasonal on weekends), Charlotte (American), Miami/Ft. Lauderdale (American and JetBlue), New York–JFK (American, Delta, JetBlue), Newark (United), Ft. Lauderdale (JetBlue, Spirit), and Philadelphia (American). Nonstop flights also arrive from both Paris (Air France) and Amsterdam (KLM) as well as Panama (Copa, which has many connections from and to the U.S.). There are also some nonstop charter flights (including some from Boston). You can also connect in San Juan on Seabourne and Winair, the St. Maarten–based local carrier. Many smaller Caribbean-based airlines, including Air Caraïbes, Anguilla Air Services, Caribbean Airlines, Air Sunshine, St. Barth Commuter, and Winair (Windward Islands Airways), offer service from other islands in the Caribbean.

AIRLINE CONTACTS Air Caraïbes. ☎ *0590/52–05–10* ⊕ *www. aircaraibes.com.* **Air Sunshine.** ✉ *Airport Rd., Simson Bay Lagoon* ☎ *954/434–8900, 800/327–8900* ⊕ *www.airsunshine.com.* **American Airlines.** ☎ *721/545–2040 Local SXM number for reservations, 800/433–7300 AA's main number* ⊕ *www.aa.com.* **Anguilla Air Services.** ✉ *Airport Rd., Simpson Bay* ☎ *264/498–5922* ⊕ *www. anguillaairservices.com.* **Caribbean Airlines.** ☎ *721/546–7610* ⊕ *www.caribbean-airlines.com.* **Copa Airlines.** ✉ *Airport Rd., Simpson Bay* ☎ *877/389–3606* ⊕ *www.copaair.com.* **Delta Airlines.** ☎ *721/546–7615, 800/221–1212* ⊕ *www.delta.com.* **JetBlue.** ☎ *721/546–7797, 877/306–4939* ⊕ *www.jetblue.com.* **St. Barth Commuter.** ☎ *0590/27–54–54* ⊕ *www.stbarthcommuter.com.*

United Airlines. ☎ 800/864–8331 ⊕ www.united.com. **Winair.** ☎ 721/545–4237 ⊕ www.fly-winair.sx.

AIRPORTS Aéroport de L'Espérance (SFG). ⊠ Rte. de l'Espérance, Grand Case ☎ 0590/27–11–00 ⊕ www.saintmartin-airport.com. **Princess Juliana International "SXM" Airport** (SXM). ☎ 721/546–. 7542 ⊕ www.sxmairport.com.

BOAT AND FERRY TRAVEL

You can take ferries to St. Barth (45–80 minutes, €55–€90 from the French side, though you can pay in dollars); to Anguilla (20 minutes, $25 from the French side); and to Saba (one to two hours, $90–$100 from the Dutch side).

CONTACTS Aqua Mania Adventures. ⊠ Simpson Bay Resort Marina Plaza, Simpson Bay ☎ 721/544–2640 ⊕ www.stmaarten-activities. com. **Great Bay Express.** ⊠ Bobby's Marina Village, Philipsburg ☎ 721/542–0032 Dutch side, 690/88–38–99 French side ⊕ www. greatbayferry.com. **Link Ferries.** ☎ 264/772–6208 ⊕ www.link.ai. **Saba Ferries.** ☎ 599/416–2299 ⊕ www.sabaferry.com. **Voyager.** ☎ 0590/87–10–68 ⊕ www.voy12.com.

CAR TRAVEL

It's easy to get around the island by car. Virtually all roads are paved and in generally good condition. However, they can be crowded, especially during high season; you might experience traffic jams, particularly around Marigot around noon and Simpson Bay from 3 pm. Be alert for occasional potholes and unpainted speed bumps (small signs warn you), as well as the island tradition of stopping in the middle of the road to chat with a friend or yield to someone entering traffic. Few roads are identified by name or number, but most have signs indicating the destination. Driving is on the right. There are gas stations all over the island, but gas tends to be cheaper on the French side.

Car Rentals: You can book a car at Princess Juliana International SXM Airport, where all major rental companies have booths, but it is often *much* cheaper to reserve a car in advance from home. That's also an especially wise move in high season when some companies' lots may run out of cars. A shuttle to the rental-car companies' lots is provided. Rates are among the best in the Caribbean, as little as $25–$40 per day in low season, but at least $240/week, and up, in high season. You can also rent a car on the French side, but this rarely makes sense for Americans because of the exchange rates.

CAR-RENTAL CONTACTS Avis. ⊠ Airport Rd., Simpson Bay ☎ 721/545–2847, 800/331–1084 ⊕ www.avis-sxm.com. **Dollar/ Thrifty Car Rental.** ⊠ 102 Airport Rd. ☎ 721/545–2393 ⊕ www.

dollarthriftysxm.com. **Empress Rent-a-Car.** ☎ 721/545–2062 ⊕ www.
empressrentacar.com. **Europcar.** ⊠ Airport Rd., Simpson Bay
☎ 721/545–3141 ⊕ www.europcar.com. **Golfe Car Rental.** ⊠ Rte.
de l'Espérance, Grand Case ☎ 0690/35–04–75 ⊕ www.golfecar-
rental.com. **Hertz.** ⊠ 82 Airport Rd., Simpson Bay ☎ 721/545–4541
⊕ www.hertz.sxmrentacar.com. **Tropical-Tropicana Car Rental.**
⊠ Onyx Rd. at Billy Folly Rd., Simpson Bay ⊹ After leaving the
airport toward Simpson Bay, turn right off Welfare Rd. at the
Hollywood Casino sign; Baker's & Tropical are on the left, opposite Atrium Resort ☎ 721/553–0571 ⊕ www.tropical-tropicana.
com. **Leisure Car Rental.** ⊠ Airport Rd., Simpson Bay ⊹ Diagonally
opposite the Winair headquarters ☎ 721/545–2359 Local office,
866/545–2359 Toll-free from U.S. ⊕ www.leisurecarrental.com.
Unity Car Rental. ⊠ 6 Sister Modesta Rd., Simpson Bay ☎ 721/520–
5767 ⊕ www.unitycarrental.com.

TAXI TRAVEL

There is a government-sponsored taxi dispatcher at the airport
and the harbor. Posted fares are for one or two people. Add $5
for each additional person, half price for kids. The first bag is free;
after that it's $1 per bag. It costs about $18 from the airport to
Philipsburg or Marigot, and about $30 to Dawn Beach. After 10
pm fares go up 25%, and after midnight 50%. Licensed drivers
can be identified by the "taxi" or new "T" license plate on the
Dutch side and the TXI license plate on the French side. Avoid
any uninsured illegal "gypsy" cabs that may appear; they have no
such plates, and police have been cracking down on them across
the island. Fixed fares apply from Juliana International Airport and
the Marigot ferry to hotels around the island.

TAXI CONTACTS Dutch St. Maarten Taxi Association. ☎ 721/543–
7814, 721/543–7815 ⊕ www.taxistmaarten.com. **Juliana Airport
Taxi Dispatch.** ☎ 721/542–1680 ⊕ www.sxmairporttaxis.com.
Marigot Taxi Dispatch. ☎ 0590/87–56–54.

Sights

The best way to explore St. Maarten/St. Martin is by car. Though
sometimes congested, especially around Philipsburg and Marigot,
the roads are fairly good, though narrow and winding, with some
speed bumps, potholes, roundabouts, and an occasional wan-
dering goat herd or stray oxen. Few roads are marked with their
names, but destination signs are somewhat common. Besides,
the island is so small that it's hard to get really lost.

If you're spending a few days, get to know the area with a scenic loop around the island. Be sure to pack a towel and some water shoes, a hat, sunglasses, and sunblock. Head up the east shoreline from Philipsburg, and follow the signs to Dawn Beach and Oyster Pond. The road winds past soaring hills, turquoise waters, quaint West Indian houses, and wonderful views of St. Barth. As you cross over to the French side, keep following the road toward Orient Bay, the St-Tropez of the Caribbean. Continue to Anse Marcel, Grand Case, and Marigot. From Marigot, the flat neighboring island of Anguilla is visible. Completing the loop through Sandy Ground and the French lowlands brings you past Cupecoy Beach, through Maho and Simpson Bay, where Saba looms on the southern horizon, and back over the mountain road into Philipsburg. A few have called it "the Great Circle Route," for good reason.

Beaches

For such a small island, St. Maarten/St. Martin has a wide array of beaches, from the long expanse of Baie Orientale on the French side to powdery-soft Mullet Bay on the Dutch side.

Several of the best Dutch-side beaches are developed and have large-scale resorts. But others, including Simpson Bay and Cupecoy, have comparatively little development. You'll sometimes find vendors or beach bars to rent chairs and umbrellas (but not always).

Almost all of the French-side beaches, whether busy Baie Orientale or less busy Baie des Pères (Friar's Bay), have beach clubs and restaurants. For about $20-$25 a couple you get two chaises (*transats*) and an umbrella (*parasol*) for the day, not to mention chair-side service for drinks and food. Only some beaches have bathrooms and showers, so if that is your preference, inquire.

Warm surf and a gentle breeze can be found at the island's 37 beaches, though breezes are generally a bit stronger on the windward Eastern shore. Every beach is open to the public. Try several. Each is unique: some bustling and some bare, some refined and some rocky, some good for snorkeling and some for sunning. Whatever your fancy, it's here, including a clothing-optional beach at the south end of beautiful Baie Orientale (Orient Beach). And several of the island's gems don't have big hotels lining their shores. Many beaches have chair rental concessions and beach bars, too. ■ TIP→ **Petty theft from cars in beach parking lots occasionally happens in the Caribbean. Leave nothing in your parked car, not even in the glove compartment or especially the trunk.**

Restaurants

Although most people come to St. Maarten/St. Martin for sun and fun, they leave praising the incredible cuisine available on both sides of the island. On an isle that covers only 37 square miles (96 square km), there are literally hundreds of restaurants. You can sample the best dishes from France, Thailand, Italy, Vietnam, India, Japan, and, of course, the Caribbean.

Some of the best restaurants are in Grand Case (on the French side), but many other fine dining restaurants now are in Simpson Bay and Porto Cupecoy, both on the Dutch side. Don't limit your culinary adventures to one area. Try the hopping upscale restaurants of Cupecoy, the tourist-friendly low-key eateries of Simpson Bay, and the many *lolos* (roadside barbecue stands) throughout. Loyalists on both "sides" will cheerfully try to steer you to their favorites. Do remember that some French-side restaurants may still offer a one-to-one exchange rate if you use cash.

During high season, it's essential to make reservations. Sometimes you can make them the same day. Dutch-side restaurants may include a 15% service charge, so check your bill before tipping. On the French side, service is usually included (worth checking, here, too), but it is customary to leave 5%–10% extra. Don't leave tips on your credit card—it's customary to tip in cash. A taxi is probably the easiest solution to the parking problems in Grand Case, Marigot, and Philipsburg. Grand Case has two pay lots—each costs several dollars—at each end of the main boulevard, and there's one well-lit free lot toward the northern end of town, which usually fills up by 8 pm. Restaurants will be happy to call you a cab to return at the end of the meal.

What to Wear: Although appropriate dining attire ranges from swimsuits to sport jackets, casual dress is usually just fine. For men, a nice shirt and pants will take you almost anywhere; for women, dressy pants, a skirt, or even fancy shorts are usually acceptable. Jeans are fine in less formal eateries.

Hotels and Resorts

The island, though small, is well developed—some say overdeveloped—and offers a wide range of lodging. The larger resorts and time shares are on the Dutch side; the French side has more intimate properties. Just keep in mind that the popular restaurants around Grand Case, on the French side, are a long drive from most Dutch-side hotels—but there are now lots of great restaurants in Simpson Bay and at Porto Cupecoy. French-side hotels charge in euros. Be wary of very low–price alternatives, short-term housing for temporary workers, or properties used by very low-end tour companies. Some locations very close to the airport can be a bit noisy.

Resorts and Time-Shares: Thanks to Hurricane Irma's destruction in 2017, virtually every SXM time-share and resort has been re-imagined from top to bottom, rebuilt better and stronger. All units are fully renovated now. There are several resorts with all-inclusive options, but before you lock yourself into a meal plan, keep in mind that restaurants at all price points are easily accessible (and that opting for an all-inclusive resort could deprive you of some seriously memorable dining experiences).

Small Inns: Small guesthouses and inns can be found on both sides of the island. It's worth considering these, especially if you are not the big-resort type. Several are quite modern and attractive, and located beachfront.

Villas and Condos: Both sides of the island have hundreds of villas and condos for every conceivable budget. Some of the resorts offer villa alternatives, which make for a good compromise, and perhaps better security. In addition, many high-end condo developments offer unsold units as rentals—and some are brand-new and terrific bargains.

Hotel reviews have been shortened. For full information, visit Fodors.com.

What It Costs in U.S. Dollars

$	$$	$$$	$$$$
RESTAURANTS			
under $12	$12–$20	$21–$30	over $30
HOTELS			
under $275	$275–$375	$376–$475	over $475

St. Maarten/St. Martin accommodations range from modern megaresorts to condos, villas, and stylish intimate guesthouses. On the Dutch side some hotels cater to groups, and although that's also true to some extent on the French side, you can find a larger collection of intimate accommodations there.
■ **TIP→ Off-season rates (April through the beginning of December) can be as little as half the high-season rates.**

Time-share properties are concentrated on the Dutch side. There's no need to buy a share, as these condos are rented out by the resorts or by time-share owners themselves whenever the owners are not in residence. If you stay in one, try to avoid a sales pitch—they can last up to two hours. Some rent by the night, but there are substantial savings if you secure a weekly rate. Not all offer daily maid service.

Villas are a great lodging option, especially for families who don't need to keep the kids occupied, or for groups of friends who like hanging out together. Since these are for the most part free-standing houses, their greatest advantage is privacy. Properties are scattered throughout the island, often in gated communities or on secluded roads. Although a few have bare-bones furnishings, most are quite luxurious, sometimes with gyms, theaters, game rooms, and several different pools. There are private chefs, gardeners, maids, and other staffers to care for both the villa and its occupants.

Villas are secured through rental companies. They offer weekly prices that range from reasonable to more than many people make in a year. Check around, as prices for the same property vary from agent to agent. Rental companies usually provide airport transfers and concierge service, and for an extra fee will even stock your refrigerator.

HomeAway
This listing service is the world's leading vacation rentals marketplace. To rent a condo, you contact the owner directly. ⊕ *www.homeaway.com*.

Island Properties
This company's properties are scattered around the island. ✉ *62 Welfare Rd., Simpson Bay* ☎ *721/544–4580, 866/978–5851 in U.S.* ⊕ *www.remaxislandproperties.com*.

Island Real Estate Team / IRE Vacations
Island Real Estate Team and its IRE Vacations division offer both sales and rentals of villas, condominiums, businesses, property, and more on both the French and Dutch sides of SXM. ✉ *91-b Welfare Rd., Simpson Bay* ☎ *721/544–4240* ⊕ *www.ireteam.com*.

Jennifer's Vacation Villas
Jennifer's specializes in vacation villas across the island, handling both short- and long-term rentals as well as villa purchases. ✉ *Plaza del Lago, Welfare Rd., Simpson Bay* ☎ *721/544–3107* ✎ *info@jennifersvacationvillas.com*.

St. Maarten Sotheby's International Realty

St. Maarten Sotheby's International Realty sells and rents luxury villas, many in gated communities. ⊠ *One Cupecoy, 1 Niger Rd., Cupecoy* ☎ *721/545–3626* ⊕ *stmartinsir.com.*

St. Martin Sotheby's International Realty

Owned by American Leslie Reed and associated with Sotheby's, this company rents upscale St. Martin villas. First-rate properties are available in all sizes and prices. The Dutch side incarnation of this business is under the same ownership. ⊠ *Plaza Caraibes Bat A Rue Kennedy, Marigot* ☎ *0590/51–02–85, 213/805–0840 in U.S.* ⊕ *www.stmartinsothebysrealty.com.*

Villas of Distinction

This company rents villas worldwide. ☎ *800/289–0900 in U.S.* ⊕ *www.villasofdistinction.com.*

WIMCO

This outfit has more hotel, villa, apartment, and condo listings in the Caribbean than many, and it has over 30 years of experience. ☎ *401/239–0319 in U.S., 888/966–8426 toll-free* ⊕ *www.wimco. com.*

Nightlife

St. Maarten has lots of evening and late-night action. To find out what's going on, pick up *St. Maarten Nights,* distributed free in the tourist office and hotels, or the Thursday edition of *The Daily Herald,* the Dutch-side newspaper. The glossy *Discover St. Martin/ St. Maarten* magazine, also free, has articles on island history and on the newest shops, discos, and restaurants.

The island's many casinos are only on the Dutch side. All have craps, blackjack, roulette, and slot machines. You must be 18 or older to gamble. Dress is casual (but not bathing suits or skimpy beachwear). Most casinos are in hotels, but there are also some that are free-standing; all are open to the public.

Shopping

Shopaholics are drawn to the array of stores—and jewelry, watches, and high-end handbags in particular are big business on both sides of the island, with the greatest concentration of jewelers on Front Street in Philipsburg. Start at the center of town near the historic Court House on Front Street. Many of the best stores are closest to the Court House. In addition, duty-free shops can offer substantial savings—about 15% to 30% below U.S. and Canadian prices—on cameras, liquor, cigars, and designer clothing, but prices are not always better, so make sure you know U.S. prices beforehand—and bargain hard. Stick with the big vendors that advertise in the tourist press to get the best quality. Be alert for idlers: they've been known on rare occassions to snatch unwatched purses.

Prices are in dollars on the Dutch side, and in euros on the French side. More bargains are to be had on the Dutch side; prices on the French side may be higher than back home, and prices in euros don't help. Merchandise may not be from the newest collections, especially with regard to clothing, but there are items available on the French side that are not available on the Dutch side.

Weddings

There's a three-day waiting period on the Dutch side—but wait, it's worse: paperwork may take several weeks to process, so be sure your venue or wedding planner has a couple of months (preferably) to get everything done for you. Yes, you can do a memorable tropical wedding on a beach, but no, you can't possibly do it tomorrow. Getting married on the French side is not a viable option because of long residency requirements.

St. Maarten (Dutch Side)

Philipsburg

The capital of Dutch St. Maarten stretches about a mile (1½ km) along an isthmus between Great Bay and the Salt Pond and has five parallel streets. Most of the village's dozens of shops and restaurants are on Front Street, narrow and cobblestone, closest to Great Bay. It can be congested when cruise ships are in port because of its many duty-free shops and several casinos, but on the busiest days, it's closed off to vehicular traffic so Front Street becomes a pleasant pedestrian mall. Little lanes called *steegjes* connect Front Street with Back Street, where locals shop for clothes and sundries. Along the beach is a ½-mile-long (1-km-long) boardwalk with restaurants, souvenir shops, and beach concessions where you can rent chairs and umbrellas for about $20, sometimes with cold drinks included. There are many Wi-Fi hot spots. The boardwalk—technically called the "Great Bay Beach Promenade"—is being further extended at its eastern end all the way to the Cruise &

Cargo Facilities, which will make for a much more scenic and enjoyable walk from the port to downtown Philipsburg.

Sights

St. Maarten Museum
MUSEUM | Hosting rotating cultural exhibits that address the history, industry, geology, and archaeology of the island, the museum contains artifacts ranging from Arawak pottery shards to objects salvaged from the wreck of HMS *Proselyte*. An interesting exhibit about hurricanes focuses on Hurricane Luis, which devastated the island in 1995. There is a good reference and video library as well. ⊠ *7 Front St., Philipsburg* ☎ *721/542–4917* 🎟 *Free.*

★ Yoda Guy Movie Exhibit
MUSEUM | **FAMILY** | This odd-sounding exhibit is actually a nonprofit museum run by Nick Maley, a movie-industry artist who was involved in the creation of Yoda and other icons. You can learn how the artist worked while enjoying the models and memorabilia on display—a must-see for *Star Wars* fans but of interest to most movie buffs. Maley is often on-hand and is happy to answer questions as time allows, and to autograph souvenirs for sale. ⊠ *19a Front St., Philipsburg* ☎ *721/542–4009.*

 Beaches

Great Bay
BEACH—SIGHT | This bustling white-sand beach curves around Philipsburg just behind Front Street, making it easy to find. Here you'll find boutiques, eateries, a pleasant boardwalk, and rental chairs and umbrellas. Busy with cruise-ship passengers, the beach is best west of Captain Hodge Pier or around Antoine Restaurant. **Amenities:** food and drink. **Best for:** swimming; walking. ⊠ *Philipsburg.*

🍴 Restaurants

Ocean Lounge
$$$$ | **ECLECTIC** | **FAMILY** | An airy modern verandah perched on the Philipsburg boardwalk gives a distinct South Beach vibe. You'll want to linger over fresh fish and steaks as you watch tourists pass by on romantic strolls by night or determined cruise-ship passengers surveying the surrounding shops by day. **Known for:** gathering place for Philipsburg movers and shakers; beachfront lounge; easy place to relax and people-watch. ⑤ *Average main: $34* ⊠ *Holland House Beach Hotel, 45 Front St., Philipsburg* ☎ *721/542–2572* ⊕ *www.hhbh.com.*

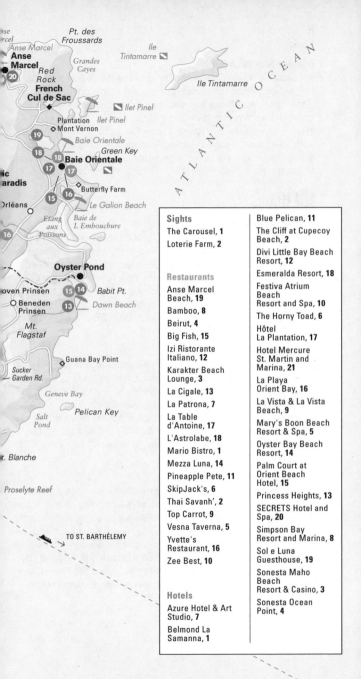

Anse Marcel
Pt. des Froussards
Ile Tintamarre
Grandes Cayes
Red Rock
French Cul de Sac
Ilet Pinel
Plantation Mont Vernon
Ilet Pinel
Baie Orientale
Green Key
Baie Orientale
Butterfly Farm
Orléans
Le Galion Beach
Etang aux Poissons
Baie de L. Embouchure
Oyster Pond
oven Prinsen
Babit Pt.
Beneden Prinsen
Dawn Beach
Mt. Flagstaf
Guana Bay Point
Sucker Garden Rd.
Geneve Bay
Salt Pond
Pelican Key
t. Blanche
Proselyte Reef
TO ST. BARTHÉLEMY

ATLANTIC OCEAN

Sights
The Carousel, **1**
Loterie Farm, **2**

Restaurants
Anse Marcel Beach, **19**
Bamboo, **8**
Beirut, **4**
Big Fish, **15**
Izi Ristorante Italiano, **12**
Karakter Beach Lounge, **3**
La Cigale, **13**
La Patrona, **7**
La Table d'Antoine, **17**
L'Astrolabe, **18**
Mario Bistro, **1**
Mezza Luna, **14**
Pineapple Pete, **11**
SkipJack's, **6**
Thai Savanh', **2**
Top Carrot, **9**
Vesna Taverna, **5**
Yvette's Restaurant, **16**
Zee Best, **10**

Hotels
Azure Hotel & Art Studio, **7**
Belmond La Samanna, **1**

Blue Pelican, **11**
The Cliff at Cupecoy Beach, **2**
Divi Little Bay Beach Resort, **12**
Esmeralda Resort, **18**
Festiva Atrium Beach Resort and Spa, **10**
The Horny Toad, **6**
Hôtel La Plantation, **17**
Hotel Mercure St. Martin and Marina, **21**
La Playa Orient Bay, **16**
La Vista & La Vista Beach, **9**
Mary's Boon Beach Resort & Spa, **5**
Oyster Bay Beach Resort, **14**
Palm Court at Orient Beach Hotel, **15**
Princess Heights, **13**
SECRETS Hotel and Spa, **20**
Simpson Bay Resort and Marina, **8**
Sol e Luna Guesthouse, **19**
Sonesta Maho Beach Resort & Casino, **3**
Sonesta Ocean Point, **4**

Taloula's Blue Bitch Bar

$$ | **ECLECTIC** | **FAMILY** | Ribs and burgers are the specialty at this casual beachfront restaurant, but the jerk chicken and thin-crust pizza, not to mention a few vegetarian items, are not to be ignored. Lunch is accompanied by (warning: loud) live music; every Friday a DJ spins tunes. **Known for:** location on the Philipsburg boardwalk; delicious tapas; entertainment night and day. ⑤ *Average main: $19* ⊠ *Sint Rose Arcade, Philipsburg* ✛ *Off Front St. on the boardwalk* ☎ *721/542–1645* ⊕ *www.bluebitchbar.com.*

🛏 Hotels

Holland House Beach Hotel

$$ | **HOTEL** | This hotel is in an ideal location for shoppers and sun worshippers; it faces Front Street and to the rear are the boardwalk and a long stretch of Great Bay Beach. **Pros:** easy access to beach and shops; free Wi-Fi; in the heart of Philipsburg. **Cons:** busy downtown location can be noisy; no pool; getting there by car is challenging when many cruise ships visit. ⑤ *Rooms from: $275* ⊠ *45 Front St., Philipsburg* ☎ *721/542–2572* ⊕ *www.hhbh. com* ➷ *48 rooms* ⦿ *Breakfast.*

Pasanggrahan Royal Inn

$ | **B&B/INN** | One of the few remaining authentic West Indian properties on St. Maarten is steeped in history; in fact, the island's oldest hotel once served as the governor's mansion. **Pros:** in the heart of Philipsburg; historic; inexpensive. **Cons:** on the main drag, which can be loaded with people; beach can be crowded; street side can be noisy. ⑤ *Rooms from: $154* ⊠ *15 Front St., Philipsburg* ☎ *721/542–3588* ⊕ *www.pasanhotel.net* ➷ *18 rooms* ⦿ *No meals.*

Sea Palace Resort

$ | **RENTAL** | **FAMILY** | This hotel and time-share, which is right on the beach in Philipsburg, is painted an eye-popping shade of coral that is hard to miss. **Pros:** walking distance to shopping; recently renovated thanks to Hurricane Irma; on Great Bay beach and the Promenade (boardwalk). **Cons:** area is crowded when cruise ships dock; not much for kids to do; can be a bit noisy during the day due to traffic. ⑤ *Rooms from: $180* ⊠ *147 Front St., Philipsburg* ☎ *721/542–2700, 800/969–1805* ⊕ *www.seapalaceresort.com* ➷ *32 units* ⦿ *No meals.*

🍸 Nightlife

★ Ocean Lounge

BARS/PUBS | Sip a guavaberry colada, and sample tapas with your chair pointed toward the boardwalk at this popular, genuinely Caribbean people-watching venue. There's free parking for patrons until midnight; enter on Back Street, and look for the Holland House banner. ☒ *Holland House Beach Hotel, 43 Front St., Philipsburg* ☎ *721/542–2572* ⊕ *www.hhbh.com.*

🛍 Shopping

Philipsburg's **Front Street** reinvented itself several years ago and continues to evolve. Now it's mall-like, with a redbrick walk and streets, some palm trees lining the sleek boutiques, jewelry stores, souvenir shops, and outdoor restaurants. Here and there a school or a church appears to remind visitors there's much more to this island than shopping. On Back Street, the **Philipsburg Market Place** is a daily open-air market where you can haggle on handicrafts, souvenirs, and beachwear. **Old Street,** off Front Street, has little stores, boutiques, and island mementos.

Ballerina Jewelers

JEWELRY/ACCESSORIES | One of the most popular jewelry stores on the island, Ballerina has jewelry by Tacori and Pandora, and watches by Bell & Ross, Technomarine, Franck Muller, and other luxury brands. ☒ *56 Front St., Philipsburg* ☎ *721/542–4399* ⊕ *www. ballerina-jewelers.com.*

★ Caribbean Gems

JEWELRY/ACCESSORIES | One of St. Maarten's oldest and most popular jewelers, Caribbean Gems has two Philipsburg locations, at both 22 and 40 Front Street, an easy walk especially for cruise ship passengers. The store features one-of-a-kind jewelry and watches in all price ranges, including many sold exclusively there. Known for impeccable customer service, Caribbean Gems has a wide selection and competitive pricing. ☒ *22 Front St. and 40 Front St.* ☎ *800/848–7925.*

Guavaberry Emporium

WINE/SPIRITS | Visitors come for free samples at the small factory where the Sint Maarten Guavaberry Company sells its famous liqueur. The many versions include one made with jalapeño peppers. Check out the hand-painted bottles. The store also sells a gourmet barbecue and hot sauce collection and souvenir hats. ☒ *8–10 Front St., Philipsburg* ☎ *721/542–2965* ⊕ *www.guavaberry.com.*

Little Europe

JEWELRY/ACCESSORIES | Come here to buy fine jewelry, crystal, and china; they carry many top brands. They have two stores in Philipsburg on 2 Front St. and 80 Front St., and one in Marigot on Rue de General de Gaulle. ⊠ *80 Front St., Philipsburg* ☎ *721/542–4371* ⊕ *www.littleeurope.com.*

Little Switzerland

JEWELRY/ACCESSORIES | This large Caribbean duty-free chain sells watches, fine crystal, china, perfume, and jewelry. There are multiple locations on the island, one a Tiffany boutique. ⊠ *52 Front St., Philipsburg* ☎ *721/542–3530* ⊕ *www.littleswitzerland.com.*

Oro Diamante

JEWELRY/ACCESSORIES | Specializing in diamonds, this store carries loose diamonds, jewelry, and watches. ⊠ *62-B Front St., Philipsburg* ☎ *599/543–0342, 800/764–0884 in U.S.* ⊕ *www.oro-dia-mante.com.*

Shipwreck Shop

CRAFTS | With multiple SXM outlets, this chain stocks a little of everything: colorful hammocks, handmade jewelry, and local Guavaberry liqueur. But the main store has the largest selection. ⊠ *42 Front St., Philipsburg* ☎ *721/542–5358.*

★ Zhaveri Jewelers & Luxury

JEWELRY/ACCESSORIES | A fixture on Front Street for more than 30 years, Zhaveri moved in 2019 to a new location four times larger than its previous store. In addition to its huge selection of loose diamonds, jewelry, watches, and gifts, Zhaveri sells designer handbags including Hugo Boss, Georgio Armani, Emporio Armani, Kartell, Furla, and Carmen Sol, as well as jewelry pieces sold nowhere else on SXM. They pay no fees to cruise lines, which makes their pricing highly competitive. ⊠ *68 Front St.* ☎ *721/542–5176* ⊕ *www.zhaveri.com.*

Cupecoy

🔺 Beaches

★ Cupecoy Beach

BEACH—SIGHT | Near the Dutch-French border, this highly picturesque area of sandstone cliffs, white sand, and shoreline caves is actually a string of small beaches that come and go according to the whims of the sea. The surf can be rough, and it's a steep walk down to the beach (made easier by a new, wider cement stairway). Despite some "no nudity" signs at the

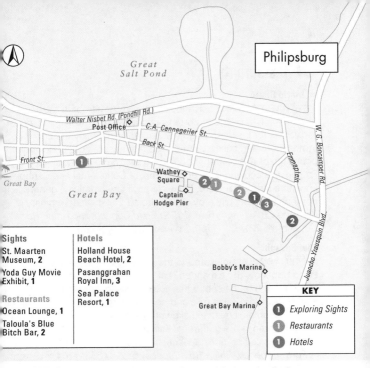

*Great
Salt Pond*

Walter Nisbet Rd. (Pondfill Rd.)
Post Office
C.A. Cannegeiter St.
Back St.
Front St.
Wathey
Square
Captain
Hodge Pier

Great Bay

Great Bay

W. G. Buoncamper Rd.

Emmaplein

Sucker Garden Rd.

Bobby's Marina

Great Bay Marina

Sights
St. Maarten
Museum, **2**
Yoda Guy Movie
Exhibit, **1**

Restaurants
Ocean Lounge, **1**
Taloula's Blue
Bitch Bar, **2**

Hotels
Holland House
Beach Hotel, **2**
Pasanggrahan
Royal Inn, **3**
Sea Palace
Resort, **1**

KEY
① Exploring Sights
① Restaurants
① Hotels

neighboring Shore Pointe condos, this beach has been "clothing optional" for decades—but wait until you're on the beach
itself before disrobing. Friendly "Dany's Cupecoy Smooth
Beach Bar," located at the top of the stairs to the beach, serves
all kinds of drinks and snacks, and sometimes fresh Caribbean
spiny lobster. It's also a superb place for meeting people who
gather here from around the world. **Amenities:** food, drink; chair
and umbrella rentals. **Best for:** relaxation; sunsets. ⊠ *Between
Baie Longue and Mullet Bay, Cupecoy.*

★ Mullet Bay Beach
BEACH—SIGHT | **FAMILY** | Many believe that this mile-long, pow-
dery white-sand beach behind the Mullet Bay Golf Course is the
island's best. You can rent umbrellas and chairs here. Swimmers
like it because the water is usually calm, but when the swell is up,
surfers take over. Be cautious here; undertow can be challenging.
Always swim with others nearby, since there are no lifeguards.
The comparatively calm cove at the south end is good for kids.
Listen for the "whispering pebbles" as the waves wash up. Beach
bars serve lunch and cold drinks. **Amenities:** food and drink. **Best
for:** families; snorkeling; surfing; swimming. ⊠ *South of Cupecoy
and Northwest of the Maho area, Mullet Bay.*

 Restaurants

★ Mario Bistro

$$$$ | ECLECTIC | FAMILY | Overlooking the yacht harbor in the Medi-terranean-style village of Porto Cupecoy, you can sit with a view of the yachts (or inside the lovely restaurant) and enjoy the convivial atmosphere and culinary excellence that ensures the ongoing popularity of this dinner spot. Though the menu is in English and French, the cooking is an eclectic mix of Continental and Caribbe-an with a little Asian flare. **Known for:** culinary creativity; generous portions (they happily provide take-home boxes); extraordinary desserts. $ *Average main: $35* ⊠ *Porto Cupecoy, 56 Rhine Rd., Cupecoy* ☎ *721/523–2760* ⊕ *www.mariobistrot.com.*

Thai Savanh'

$$ | THAI | FAMILY | Relocated to the growing culinary outpost at Porto Cupecoy, the expanded Thai Savanh' offers authentic Thai cuisine that hits the spot when you're craving something spicy and exotic. From salad rolls and *nems* (spring rolls) to delicious curries, noodle dishes, and skewered satays, the food is satisfying and the portions are generous. **Known for:** supremely tasty Thai food; well-sized portions; reasonable prices. $ *Average main: $18* ⊠ *Porto Cupecoy, Rhine Rd., Cupecoy* ☎ *721/ 553–1204* ⊙ *Closed Sun.* ▭ *No credit cards.*

🛏 Hotels

The Cliff at Cupecoy Beach

$$$ | RENTAL | These luxurious, high-rise condos are rented out when the owners are not in residence; depending on the owner's personal style, they can be downright fabulous. **Pros:** great views; good for families; close to SXM airport and Maho and Porto Cupecoy restaurants. **Cons:** limited services; traffic and some nearby construction; getting to Orient Beach or Philipsburg is a chore from here. $ *Rooms from: $425* ⊠ *Rhine Rd., Cupecoy* ☎ *866/978–5839, 721/546–6633* ⊕ *www.cliffsxm.com* ⇥ *72 units* ❙⊙❙ *No meals.*

Maho

People flock to Maho Beach to see dramatically low plane land-ings to Princess Juliana; they seem to pass just above your head. If you want to catch a glimpse, head to Sonesta Ocean Point.

Hotels

Sonesta Maho Beach Resort & Casino

$$ | RESORT | FAMILY | The island's largest hotel, which is on Maho Beach and typically caters to big groups, isn't luxurious or fancy, but its most recent post-Irma update makes it a much more vibrant, attractive property than in its pre-Irma days. **Pros:** family-friendly; lots of shopping; nonstop activities. **Cons:** large resort, not remotely intimate; not for a quiet getaway; limited (but growing) dining choices on all-inclusive plan. ⑤ *Rooms from: $283* ✉ *1 Rhine Rd., Maho Reef* ☎ *800/766–3782* ⊕ *www.sonesta.com/ mahobeach* ➩ *420 rooms* ❑ *All-inclusive.*

★ Sonesta Ocean Point

$$$$ | RESORT | The roomy suites in this sophisticated, luxurious enclave are some of the very best accommodations on the island. **Pros:** brand-new comfortable rooms; great design; private dining. **Cons:** access is through the Sonesta Maho complex; proximity to airport gives you a lot of chances to watch the dramatic plane landings, but it can be noisy during takeoffs; fairly long walk to all the Maho-area restaurants and bars (golf carts available). ⑤ *Rooms from: $744* ✉ *14 A Rhine Rd., Maho Reef* ☎ *721/545–3100* ⊕ *www.sonesta.com/oceanpoint* ➩ *219 rooms* ❑ *All-inclusive.*

🍸 Nightlife

Casino Royale

CASINOS | Completely re-imagined after being destroyed by Hurricane Irma, Casino Royale is back. It boasts more than 21,000 square feet of gaming and is home to the biggest theater on the island. With 22 tables, 400 slot machines, a private high-roller area, free Vegas-style production shows weekly, a VIP Lounge, live music, and more, it is one of the most rewarding programs in the Caribbean. ✉ *Sonesta Maho Beach Resort & Casino, 1 Rhine Rd., Maho Reef* ☎ *721/545–2590* ⊕ *www.playmaho.com.*

★ JAX Steakhouse & Cocktail Bar

$$$$ | STEAKHOUSE | Diners have been flocking to JAX for Certified Angus beef steaks since the restaurant opened in 2019. The attractive ambience and great service are a tribute to the owner's years of experience as a restaurateur on the island. **Known for:** superior quality steaks; great ambience and service to match; central location in Maho. ⑤ *Average main: $39* ✉ *Sonesta Maho Resort, 1 Rhine Rd., Maho Reef* ☎ *721/588–8884* ☾ *No lunch.*

Sunset Bar and Grill

BARS/PUBS | This popular spot near the ocean edge of the Princess Juliana SXM Airport runway offers a relaxed, anything-goes atmosphere. Watch big planes fly very low over your head a few seconds before landing, while you enjoy a BBC (Bailey's banana colada), the island's favorite tropical drink, or a bucket of beers. Bring your camera for stunning photos, but expect a high noise level. Note: drinks here can be quite pricey. There's occasional entertainment at night. ⊠ *Maho Beach, Beacon Hill # 2, Maho Reef* ☎ *721/545–2084.*

Oyster Pond

Beaches

Dawn Beach

BEACH—SIGHT | True to its name, this is a great place to be at sunrise with your camera. Located on the Atlantic side of Oyster Pond, just south of the French border, it's a first-class beach for sunning and snorkeling, but the winds and rough water mean only strong swimmers should attempt to take a dip (there are no lifeguards). It's not usually crowded, and there are still some good restaurants in the area, though some were destroyed by Hurricane Irma and will not return. Locals often fish here in early mornings or evenings—as do brown pelicans. To find the beach, follow the signs to Oyster Bay Beach Resort, Big Fish Restaurant, or Dawn Beach Club. **Amenities:** food and drink. **Best for:** snorkeling (particularly at the northern end); sunrise. ⊠ *South of Oyster Pond, Dawn Beach.*

🍽 Restaurants

★ Big Fish

$$$ | **ECLECTIC** | **FAMILY** | Big Fish offers big portions of fresh-caught fish, sushi, and upscale steaks served in a modern, Miami Beach atmosphere. The service is friendly and attentive. **Known for:** South Beach vibes; spicy Hurricane shrimp; great service. $ *Average main: $28* ⊠ *14 Emerald Merit Rd., Oyster Pond* ☎ *721/543–6288.*

Hotels

Oyster Bay Beach Resort

$ | **RESORT** | **FAMILY** | Jutting out into the Atlantic and Oyster Pond, this condo/time-share resort sits overlooking Dawn Beach and is convenient to groceries, restaurants, and Dawn Beach Club down the road. **Pros:** lots of activities; nightly entertainment; very comfortable accommodations. **Cons:** isolated location; need a car to get around; many area restaurants closed after Irma. $ *Rooms from: $150* ✉ *10 Emerald Merit Rd., Oyster Pond* ☎ *721/543–6040* ⊕ *www.oysterbaybeachresort.com* ⇥ *157 units* ❍ *No meals.*

Princess Heights
$ | **RENTAL** | Perched on a hill hundreds of feet above the Atlantic, renovated, spacious suites offer privacy, luxury, and white-balustrade balconies with a smashing view of St. Barth. **Pros:** away from the crowds; friendly staff; gorgeous vistas. **Cons:** not on the beach and need a car to get around; numerous steps to climb in the older building; not easy to find. $ *Rooms from: $228* ✉ *156 Oyster Pond Rd., Oyster Pond* ☎ *800/881–1744* ⊕ *www.princessheights.com* ⇥ *51 suites* ❍ *No meals.*

Pelican Key

🍴 Restaurants

★ La Patrona
$$ | **MEXICAN** | Simpson Bay Resort's seaside Mexican restaurant delivers on authenticity (as in, you won't find any Tex-Mex here). Dine indoors or outside for views of the bay, whether you're here for breakfast, lunch, dinner, or happy hour. **Known for:** seafood enchiladas; some of the best pizza on the island; live music. $ *Average main: $20* ✉ *Billy Folly Rd., Pelican Key* ☎ *721/544-2503.*

🛏 Hotels

★ Blue Pelican
$$ | **RENTAL** | The 13 modern and chic apartment units hidden in this private enclave in Pelican Key were built by the owners of Hotel L'Esplanade and Le Petit Hotel, on the French side, and share the management's vision, graciousness, almost obsessive attention to detail, and concern for guest comfort and safety. **Pros:** nicest place in the area; great pool; excellent management and security. **Cons:** seven-night minimum; not on the beach; no restaurant, but several are fairly close. $ *Rooms from: $290* ✉ *Billy Folly Rd., Pelican Key* ☎ *0690/50–60–20* ⊕ *www.bluepelicansxm.com* ⇥ *13 units* ❍ *No meals.*

Festiva Atrium Beach Resort and Spa
$ | **RENTAL** | **FAMILY** | Lush tropical foliage in the glassed-in lobby—hence the name—makes a great first impression at this good base for island explorations. **Pros:** family-friendly environment;

short walk to restaurants and close to the beach; free shuttle to Philipsburg. **Cons:** rooms lack private balconies; neighborhood is crowded; taxes and service charges add a whopping 25% to basic rates. ⑤ *Rooms from: $215* ⊠ *6 Billy Folly Rd., Pelican Key* ☎ *888/992–8748* ⊕ *www.festiva-atrium.com* ⇆ *87 rooms* ⦿ *No meals.*

★ Simpson Bay Resort and Marina

$ | RENTAL | FAMILY | Tucked away on Pelican Key, the renovated Simpson Bay Resort borders both the bay and the ocean, giving you a front-row seat for island sunsets from your terrace. **Pros:** family-friendly resort on the beach; close to restaurants and nightlife options; close to SXM airport. **Cons:** maid service only weekly; busy area; main cities are each at least 20 minutes away in perfect conditions. ⑤ *Rooms from: $208* ⊠ *7 Billy Folly Rd., Pelican Key* ☎ *888/721–4407, 954/736–5807* ⊕ *www.simpsonbayresort. com* ⇆ *342 units* ⦿ *No meals.*

Simpson Bay

Sights

★ The Carousel

CAROUSEL | FAMILY | After riding this beautiful restored Italian carousel in the heart of Simpson Bay, kids of all ages can enjoy dozens of flavors of homemade gelato, an engaging photo exhibit of famous people eating ice cream, and a carousel museum with great souvenirs. ⊠ *60 Welfare Rd., Cole Bay* ☎ *721/544–3112* 🎟 *$2.*

🏖 Beaches

★ Simpson Bay Beach

BEACH—SIGHT | This half-moon stretch of white sand on the island's Caribbean side is a hidden gem. It's mostly surrounded by private residences, with no big resorts, few Jet Skiers, and no crowds. It's just you, the sand, and the water (along with one funky beach bar, Karakter, at the beach's northern end, to provide some chairs and nourishment). The beach is sometimes a bit noisy when planes depart nearby. To the south, on Old Simpson Bay Road, look for the tiny new Guayabera Beach Club, open daily for breakfast and lunch and nightly with different music, ranging from steel pan to jazz. To find the beach, follow the signs southeast of the airport to Mary's Boon and the Horny Toad guesthouses.

Amenities: food and drink; showers; toilets. **Best for:** solitude; swimming; walking. ⊠ *Simpson Bay.*

🍽 Restaurants

★ Bamboo

$$$ | **ASIAN FUSION** | With a new location on Simpson Bay, Bamboo continues its 15-plus year tradition of blending contemporary Latin and Asian flavors with more complexity and innovation than ever. While old favorites like their Angry Dragon Roll, the Kuta Roll, and the Maui Wowi Roll remain, they've added new items like miso-glazed short rib lettuce wraps and Bamboo tacos with chorizo. **Known for:** sushi and sashimi; dynamic, upbeat ambience; innovative menu. ⑤ *Average main: $27* ⊠ *Puerta del Sol, Welfare Rd., Simpson Bay* ☎ *721/544–2693* ⊕ *www.bamboo-sxm.com.*

Beirut

$ | **LEBANESE** | **FAMILY** | Beirut serves delicious, fresh Middle Eastern specialties such as falafel, kebabs, and salads, as well as meze such as baba ghanoush. The friendly owners make everyone feel right at home, and there's a hookah bar in the back in the evening. **Known for:** casual, welcoming atmosphere; friendly staff; reasonable prices. ⑤ *Average main: $11* ⊠ *29 Airport Rd., Simpson Bay* ☎ *721/545–3612.*

★ Izi Ristorante Italiano

$$$ | **ITALIAN** | **FAMILY** | The award-winning former chef and owner of La Gondola serves up sharable portions of more than 400 dishes in this popular, cheerful, centrally located space. For something fun, diners are invited to create their own menu: pick a pasta and sauce, then add your choice of meat, fish, and veggies. **Known for:** creative, hands-on chef; unequaled tasting menu; homemade desserts that are worth saving room for. ⑤ *Average main: $23* ⊠ *Paradise Mall, 67 Welfare Rd., Simpson Bay* ☎ *721/544–3079* ⊕ *www.izirestaurant.com* ⊗ *Closed Tues.*

★ Karakter Beach Lounge

$$$ | **ECLECTIC** | **FAMILY** | This funky and charming modern beach bar, right behind the airport, serves up fun, great music, relaxation, and a lot of style. The vibe is more like St-Tropez than St. Maarten. **Known for:** funky surroundings (an old school bus); good food; on the beach. ⑤ *Average main: $21* ⊠ *121 Simpson Bay Rd., Simpson Bay* ☎ *721/523–9983* ⊕ *www.karakterstmaarten.com.*

Pineapple Pete

$$ | **SEAFOOD** | **FAMILY** | This long-popular, casual, and fun (if touristy) place is well located and has a game room with seven pool tables, four dart boards, a newly expanded arcade, and some flat-screen

TVs tuned to sports. A friendly, efficient staff serves up burgers, seafood, and ribs. **Known for:** lobster thermidor; reasonable prices; generous portions. ⑤ *Average main: $20* ✉ *56 Welfare Rd., Simpson Bay* ☎ *721/544–6030* ⊕ *www.pineapplepete.com.*

★ SkipJack's
$$$ | SEAFOOD | FAMILY | Arguably the island's top seafood restaurant, SkipJack's is located right on Simpson Bay lagoon. It is popular for crowd-pleasers such as its fried calamari, shrimp cocktail, sandwiches, and a good variety of fresh seafood. **Known for:** lobster from Saba; one of the biggest and busiest SXM restaurants; seasoned, friendly, knowledgeable staff. ⑤ *Average main: $21* ✉ *Welfare Rd., Simpson Bay* ☎ *721/ 544–2313* ⊕ *www. skipjacks-sxm.com.*

★ Top Carrot
$ | VEGETARIAN | FAMILY | Open from 7:30 am to 6 pm, this friendly café and juice bar is a popular healthy breakfast and lunch stop. It features fresh and tasty vegetarian entrées, sandwiches, salads, and homemade pastries. **Known for:** crowd-pleasing menu; casual, cozy little dining room; great gift shop. ⑤ *Average main: $9* ✉ *Airport Rd., near Simpson Bay Yacht Club, Simpson Bay* ☎ *721/544–3381* ۞ *Closed Sun. No dinner.*

★ Vesna Taverna
$$ | ECLECTIC | FAMILY | Centrally located just north of the Simpson Bay drawbridge, this casual restaurant is open all day long, with French and Mediterranean specials nightly and incredible homemade desserts. In the morning, you can order American breakfasts (including their famous Bagel Tower, plus omelets, pancakes, and more), and at lunch they offer tasty but healthy options like smoothies, sandwiches, salads, and burgers. **Known for:** Greek specialties; homemade bagels; delicious homemade desserts. ⑤ *Average main: $15* ✉ *9 La Palapa Marina, Simpson Bay* ⊹ *In front of Soggy Dollar Bar on Simpson Bay lagoon* ☎ *721/524–5283* ⊕ *www.vesnataverna.com* ۞ *No dinner Sun. and Mon. Closed Tues. in low season.*

Zee Best
$ | CAFÉ | This friendly bistro serves one of the most popular breakfasts on the island. There's a huge selection of fresh-baked pastries—try the almond croissants—plus sweet and savory crepes, omelets, quiches, and other treats from the oven. **Known for:** pastry basket; breakfast served until 2; St. Martin omelet. ⑤ *Average main: $8* ✉ *Plaza del Lago, Simpson Bay* ☎ *721/544–2477* ⊕ *www.zeebestrestaurant.com* ⊟ *No credit cards* ۞ *No dinner.*

Hotels

Azure Hotel & Art Studio

$ | HOTEL | FAMILY | Azure is a funky, wonderful boutique hotel located on a serene stretch of Simpson Bay Beach. **Pros:** central location; inexpensive; on the beach. **Cons:** no pool; no on-site restaurant (but there are kitchenettes); a car is needed to get to Philipsburg or the French side. $ *Rooms from: $90* ⊠ *6 Roberts Dr., Simpson Bay* ☎ *721/581–3858* ⊕ *www.azurehotelsxm.com* ⤶ *8 rooms* ⏐○⏐ *No meals.*

★ The Horny Toad

$ | B&B/INN | Because of its stupendous view of Simpson Bay and the simple but comfortable rooms with creative decor, this lovely guesthouse (fully rebuilt after Hurricane Irma) is widely considered one of the best on this side of the island. **Pros:** tidy rooms; friendly vibe and fantastic owners; beautiful beach that's usually deserted. **Cons:** need a car to get around; no kids under seven; no pool (but you're on the beach). $ *Rooms from: $130* ⊠ *2 Vlaun Dr., Simpson Bay* ☎ *721/545–4323* ⊕ *www.thtgh.com* ⤶ *8 rooms* ⏐○⏐ *No meals.*

La Vista & La Vista Beach

$ | RENTAL | FAMILY | Hibiscus and bougainvillea line brick walkways that connect the bungalows and beachfront suites of this intimate and friendly, family-owned time-share resort perched at the foot of Pelican Key. The accommodations, which have completed extensive post-Irma renovations, are simply but beautifully furnished and have small bathrooms, but the balconies have awesome views. **Pros:** close to restaurants and bars; nearest good beach is at Simpson Bay Resort; very walkable; centrally located. **Cons:** no-frills furnishings; beach is a bit rocky; nothing fancy. $ *Rooms from: $220* ⊠ *53 Billy Folly Rd., Simpson Bay* ☎ *721/544–3005* ⊕ *www.lavistaresort.com* ⤶ *50 units* ⏐○⏐ *No meals.*

Mary's Boon Beach Resort & Spa

$ | HOTEL | FAMILY | A shaded courtyard welcomes guests at this quirky, informal guesthouse on a 3-mile-long (5-km-long) stretch of Simpson Bay Beach, which has the funky feel of the Florida Keys. **Pros:** small and intimate; interesting history; owners are usually on-site. **Cons:** need a car; because of airport proximity, it can be noisy during takeoffs; basic bathrooms. $ *Rooms from: $135* ⊠ *117 Simpson Bay Rd., Simpson Bay* ☎ *721/545–7000* ⊕ *www. marysboon.com* ⤶ *37 rooms* ⏐○⏐ *No meals.*

Nightlife

Buccaneer Beach Bar

BARS/PUBS | Conveniently located on Kim Sha Beach in Simpson Bay, this family-friendly bar can provide you a BBC (Bailey's banana colada), a slice of pizza, a sunset, and a nightly fireball show. It's popular with both tourists and locals. Their small parking lot fills quickly; there is some on-street parking near the entrance, but parking can be a huge challenge here. ⊠ *10 Billy Folly Rd., behind Festiva Atrium Beach Resort, Simpson Bay* ☎ *721/522–9700* ⊕ *www.buccaneerbeachbar.com.*

Paradise Plaza Casino & Sports Book

CASINOS | Part of the same organization that operates the Starz City casino in Cupecoy, Paradise Plaza attracts a mostly local crowd despite being located in the Simpson Bay tourist area. Betting on sporting events is the big thing at Paradise Plaza, which explains the 20 TVs tuned to whatever game happens to be on. There are also about 250 slots and multigame machines. ⊠ *69 Welfare Rd., Simpson Bay* ☎ *721/543–4721.*

Pineapple Pete

BARS/PUBS | **FAMILY** | You can groove to live music or hit the game room for a couple of rounds of pool or video games. ⊠ *Airport Rd., Simpson Bay* ☎ *721/544–6030* ⊕ *www.pineapplepete.com.*

The Red Piano

BARS/PUBS | One of SXM's first Piano Bars, The Red Piano remains one of the island's most popular entertainment venues. It is located in the heart of Simpson Bay Resort and has live music nightly, tasty cocktails, and a pool table. Smoking is permitted. ⊠ *35 Billy Folly Rd., Simpson Bay* ☎ *721/527–4266* ⊕ *www.theredpianosxm.com.*

Little Bay

Beaches

★ Little Bay

BEACH—SIGHT | Despite its occasional use by snorkelers, divers, kayakers, and boating enthusiasts, Little Bay isn't usually crowded. It does boast panoramic views of neighboring islands St. Eustatius (Statia) and Saba, and arriving and departing cruise ships. The beach is on the same peninsula as Fort Amsterdam and accessible only via the Divi Little Bay Beach Resort, and most beachgoers are hotel guests. **Amenities:** food and drink at the resort; parking; toilets. **Best for:** snorkeling; swimming; walking. ⊠ *Little Bay Rd., Little Bay.*

🛏 Hotels

★ Divi Little Bay Beach Resort

$ | **RESORT** | **FAMILY** | Bordering gorgeous Little Bay, this growing, just-renovated property is centrally located and awash with water sports, new restaurants, and an awesome new multilevel pool with breathtaking views of neighboring islands. **Pros:** good location; lovely beach with nearby restaurants; completely renovated. **Cons:** some construction in the area; inconvenient entrance from the main road; car necessary to venture off-site. 💲 *Rooms from: $215* ✉ *Little Bay Rd., Little Bay* 📞 *721/542–2333* ⊕ *www.divilittlebay.com* 🛏 *218 rooms* ❍❙ *No meals; All-inclusive.*

🏃 Activities

BOATING AND SAILING

The water and winds are perfect for skimming the surf. It'll cost you around $1,200 to $1,500 per day to rent a 28- to 40-foot powerboat, considerably less for smaller boats or small sailboats. Drinks and sometimes lunch are usually included on crewed day charters, and some tours are eco-oriented.

★ Enigma C3 by Neil Roebert

BOATING | **FAMILY** | Seasoned Captain Neil Roebert sailed to St. Maarten from South Africa in the mid-'90s and has been doing day charters and scheduled trips around SXM and to nearby islands ever since. His most popular is a full day trip to the beautiful uninhabited island of Tintamarre, including beach time, snorkeling off Creole Rock, a full lunch, and an open bar. Many of his passengers are repeat visitors who take trips with him year after year. ✉ *Simpson Bay* 📞 *721/526–1170 Capt. Neil's cell phone* ⊕ *sailstmaarten.com.*

Random Wind

BOATING | This company offers full-day sailing and snorkeling trips on a new catamaran, also called Random Wind, replacing their 54-foot clipper that sank during Irma. Charter prices depend on the size of the group and whether lunch is served. The regularly scheduled Paradise Daysail (10–3, $119 per person for adults, $95 kids 5–12) includes food and drink, snorkeling equipment, and stand-up paddleboard. Departures, weekdays at 9:45, are from near the cruise ship terminal in Philipsburg or from Simpson Bay, by prearrangement. Everyone loves "flying" from the Tarzan swing. ■**TIP**➔ **You can get the best rates from the website rather than hotels or cruises.** ✉ *Simpson Bay* 📞 *721/587–5742* ⊕ *www. randomwind.com.*

Rhino Safari

BOATING | Take a 2½-hour guided water tour around the island on a 10-foot inflatable watercraft. The boats are stable, easy to pilot, and riding the waves is a blast. The tour includes 45 minutes of snorkeling (equipment provided) at Creole Rock, the best snorkeling spot on the island. Choose from several departures and routes every day. ✉ *58 Welfare Rd., Simpson Bay* ☎ *721/544–3150* ⊕ *www.rhinorides.com* 🖅 *From $75 per person.*

St. Maarten 12-Metre Challenge

BOATING | Sailing experience is not necessary as participants compete on 68-foot racing yachts, including Dennis Connor's *Stars and Stripes* (the actual boat that won the America's Cup in Freemantle, Australia, in 1987), *Canada II,* and *True North I.* Everyone is allocated a crew position, either grinding winches, trimming sails, punching the stopwatch, or bartending. The thrill is priceless, but book well in advance; this is one of the most popular shore excursions in the Caribbean. It is offered up to four times daily and lasts 2½–3 hours. Children over 12 (7 with sailing experience) may participate. ✉ *Bobby's Marina, Philipsburg* ☎ *721/542–0045* ⊕ *www.12metre.com.*

DIVING

Diving in St. Maarten/St. Martin has become a major attraction, with reef expeditions and sunken boats easily accessible offshore. The seawater temperature here is rarely below 78°F and visibility is often 60 to 100 feet. The island has more than 30 dive sites, from wrecks to rocky labyrinths. Right outside Philipsburg, 55 feet under the water, is the HMS *Proselyte,* once explored by Jacques Cousteau. Although it sank in 1801, the boat's cannons and coral-encrusted anchors are still visible.

Off the northwest coast, in the protected and mostly current-free Grand Case Bay, is **Creole Rock.** The water here ranges in depth from 10 feet to 25 feet. Other sites off the northern coast include **Ilet Pinel,** with shallow diving; **Green Key,** with its vibrant barrier reef; and **Tintamarre,** with its sheltered coves and geologic faults. On average, one-tank dives start at $65; two-tank dives are about $115. Certification courses start at about $450.

The Dutch side offers several full-service outfitters and SSI (Scuba Schools International) and/or PADI certification. There are no hyperbaric chambers on the island.

Dive Safaris

SCUBA DIVING | Certified divers who have dived within the last two years can watch professional feeders give reef sharks a little nosh in a half-hour shark-awareness dive. The company also offers a full

PADI training program and can tailor dive excursions and sophisti-cated, sensitive instruction to any level. ⊠ *16 Airport Rd., Simpson Bay* ☎ *721/545–2401* ⊕ *www.divesafarisstmaarten.com.*

Ocean Explorers Dive Center

SCUBA DIVING | St. Maarten's oldest dive shop offers different types of certification courses. Serious divers like the eight-person-maxi-mum policy on trips, but this means you must reserve in advance. Have a small group? You can easily reserve the entire boat, given sufficient notice. ⊠ *113 Welfare Rd., Simpson Bay* ☎ *721/544–5252* ⊕ *www.stmaartendiving.com.*

FISHING

You can angle for yellowtail snapper, grouper, marlin, tuna, and wahoo on deep-sea excursions. Costs range from $150 per person for a half day to $250 and up for a full day. Prices usually include bait and tackle, instruction for novices, and refreshments. Ask about licensing and insurance. Most boats give you some fillets but otherwise keep the fish, so if you want to keep yours, arrange it in advance.

★ Rudy's Deep Sea Fishing

FISHING | One of the more experienced sport-angling outfits runs private charter trips. Half-day excursions for up to four people start at $595. Rudy is reasonable; you can have the fillets you need and he keeps the rest. ■**TIP**→ **Check the website for great tips on fishing around St. Maarten.** ⊠ *14 Airport Rd., Simpson Bay* ☎ *721/545–2177* ⊕ *www.rudysdeepseafishing.com.*

GOLF

Mullet Bay Golf Course

GOLF | St. Maarten is not a golf destination. Nevertheless, this golf course is 18 holes (and the island's only choice), and offers tremendous views, though it's hardly a must-play. Good clubs are available for rent, and you can wear sneakers if you don't have golf shoes with you. If you're looking for real golf, consider Anguilla, a quick 25-minute ferry ride from Marigot (passport and port fees required). There's also a nine-hole course completing development at Loterie Farm if a good, new course and incredible scenery are appealing lures. Loterie Farm offers excellent natural food as well. Caution: wild vervet monkeys will occasionally saunter across the Loterie Farm course. ⊠ *Airport Rd., north of airport, Mullet Bay* ☎ *721/545–2850* 🖘 *$40* ⚑. *18 holes, 6200 yards, par 70.*

HORSEBACK RIDING

Lucky Stables

HORSEBACK RIDING | These stables in Cay Bay, part of a nature park, offer hour-long rides every hour on the hour. For a romantic treat, book a sunset ride with champagne and a bonfire (complete with marshmallows) for about $100 per person. All experience levels are welcome, as the horses only walk, but advanced riders can book private rides if they want to trot and canter. ⊠ *64 Cay Bay Rd., Cay Bay* ☎ *721/544–5255* ⊕ *www.seasidenaturepark.com.*

KAYAKING

Kayaking continues to be very popular and is frequently offered at the many water-sports operations on both the Dutch and the French sides. Rental starts at roughly $15–$20 per hour for a single and up to about $25 for a double.

★ TriSports

KAYAKING | FAMILY | This company has a full slate of reasonably priced kayaking activities, but they also offer bike tours. TriSports organizes leisurely 2½-hour combination kayaking and snorkeling excursions in addition to its biking and hiking tours. Prices vary but a fee of roughly $49 includes all equipment. ⊠ *Airport Rd., 14B, Simpson Bay* ☎ *721/545–4384* ⊕ *www.trisportsxm.com.*

SEA EXCURSIONS

★ Aqua Mania Adventures

BOATING | FAMILY | You can take day cruises to Prickly Pear Cay, off Anguilla, aboard the *Lambada,* or sunset and dinner cruises on the 65-foot sail catamaran *Tango. The Edge* goes to Saba and Statia. There are tours on inflatable boats, scuba and snorkel trips, and motor cruises around the island. ⊠ *Simpson Bay Resort Marina, Simpson Bay* ☎ *721/544–2640, 721/544–2631* ⊕ *www. stmaarten-activities.com.*

Arawak

BOATING | The 52-foot, competition-savvy sailing catamaran accommodates a maximum of just 12 people, enabling an intimate, enjoyable sailing experience. Bluebeard charters regular trips to points in Anguilla including Little Bay, Meads Bay, and Dog Island. Once in the bay, passengers can swim, snorkel, and enjoy the beautiful scenery. No specific sailing experience is required since a captain and crew are onboard, but passengers can assist them and experience racing in a safe and secure way. Soft drinks and beer are offered onboard. *Arawak* is built for speed! Private charters are also available. ⊠ *Billy Folly Rd. 10, Simpson Bay* ☎ *721/587–5935* ⊕ *www.bluebeardcharters.com.*

Golden Eagle III

BOATING | FAMILY | The sleek 76-foot catamaran *Golden Eagle III* takes day-sailors on eco-friendly excursions to outlying islets and reefs for snorkeling and partying. They can pick you up from your hotel or condo. The same company offers other boats and tours, including the double-deck *Explorer* for cruises in Simpson Bay Lagoon. ⊠ *Bobby's Marina, Jurancho Yrausquin Bd., Philipsburg* ☎ *721/543–0068* ⊕ *www.toursxm.com.*

SNORKELING

Some of the best snorkeling on the Dutch side can be found around the rocks below Fort Amsterdam off Little Bay Beach; in the southern end of Maho Bay, near Beacon Hill; off Pelican Key; and around the reefs off the northern end of Dawn Beach, near Oyster Bay Beach Resort. On the French side, the area around Baie Orientale—including Caye Verte (Green Key) and Tintamarre—is especially beautiful and is officially classified and protected as a regional underwater nature reserve. Sea creatures also congregate around Creole Rock at the point of Baie de Grand Case, though the shallows in that area are said to offer superior snorkeling activity. The average cost of an afternoon snorkeling trip is $45–$55 per person.

Blue Bubbles

SNORKELING | FAMILY | This company offers both boat and shore snorkel excursions as well as Jet Skiing, parasailing, and SNUBA for beginner divers. Snorkel excursions are $45 for 2 hours and $75 for four hours. ⊠ *153 Front St., Philipsburg* ☎ *721/556–8484* ⊕ *www.bluebubblessxm.com.*

St. Martin (French Side)

Marigot

It is great fun to spend a few hours exploring the harbor, shopping stalls, open-air cafés, and boutiques of French St. Martin's biggest town, especially on Wednesday and Saturday, when the daily open-air crafts markets expand to include fresh fruits and vegetables, spices, and all manner of seafood. The market might remind you of Provence, especially when aromas of delicious cooking waft by. Be sure to climb up to the fort for the panoramic view, stopping at the museum for an overview of the island. Marina Port La Royale is the shopping–lunch spot central to the port, but rue de la République and rue de la Liberté, which border the bay, have some duty-free shops and boutiques. The West Indies Mall offers a deluxe (and air-conditioned) shopping experience. There's less bustle here than in Philipsburg, but the open-air cafés are still tempting places to sit and people-watch. From the harbor front you can catch ferries to Anguilla and St. Barth. Parking can be a real challenge during the business day, and even at night during high season.

Get the best sunset view over Marigot from Fort Louis.

👁 Sights

Fort Louis

ARCHAEOLOGICAL SITE | Though not much remains of the structure itself, Fort Louis, completed by the French in 1789, is great fun if you want to climb the 92 steps to the top for the wonderful views of the island and neighboring Anguilla. On Wednesday and Saturday there is a market in the square at the bottom. ⊠ *Marigot*.

🏖 Beaches

Baie des Pères (*Friar's Bay*)

BEACH—SIGHT | **FAMILY** | This quiet, occasionally rocky cove close to Marigot has beach grills and bars, with chaises and umbrellas, usually calm waters, and a lovely view of Anguilla. Kali's Beach Bar, open daily for lunch and (weather permitting) dinner, has a Rasta vibe and color scheme. It's the best place to be on the full moon, with music, dancing, and a huge bonfire, but you can get lunch, beach chairs, and umbrellas anytime. Friar's Bay Beach Café is a French bistro on the sand, open from breakfast to sunset. To get to the beach, take National Road 7 from Marigot, go toward Grand Case to the Morne Valois hill, and turn left on the dead-end road at the sign. Note the last 200 yards of road to the beach is dirt and quite bumpy. **Amenities:** food and drink; toilets. **Best for:** partiers; swimming; walking. ⊠ *Anse des Pères*.

A Tale of Two Islands

The smallest island in the world to be shared between two different countries, St. Maarten/St. Martin has existed peacefully in its divided state for more than 370 years. The Treaty of Concordia, which subdivided the island, was signed in 1648 and was really inspired by the two resident colonies of French and Dutch settlers (not to mention their respective governments) joining forces to repel a common enemy, the Spanish, in 1644. Although the French were promised the side of the island facing Anguilla and the Dutch the south side of the island, the boundary itself wasn't firmly established until 1817 and only then after several disputes (16 of them, to be exact).

Visitors to the island will likely not be able to tell that they have passed from the Dutch to the French side unless they notice the border monuments at the side of the roads—and that roads on the French side feel a little smoother. In 2003 the population of St. Martin (and St. Barthélemy) voted to secede from Guadeloupe, the administrative capital of the French West Indies. That detachment became official in 2007, and St. Martin is now officially known as the Collectivité de Saint-Martin.

Happy Bay Beach (*Anse Heureuse*)

BEACH—SIGHT | Not many people know about this romantic, hidden gem. Happy Bay has powdery sand, a backdrop of luxury villas in the hills, and stunning views of Anguilla. The snorkeling is also good. To get here, turn onto the rather rutted dead-end road to Baie des Péres (Friar's Bay). The beach itself, which is clothing-optional, is a 10- to 15-minute walk from the northernmost beach bar on Friar's Bay. **Amenities:** food and drink; toilets (at Friar's Bay). **Best for:** snorkeling; solitude; swimming; walking. ⊠ *Happy Bay*.

 Restaurants

Bistro Nu

$$$ | FRENCH | It's hard to top the authentic French comfort food and reasonable prices you can find at this intimate restaurant tucked in a Marigot alley. Traditional French dishes like steak au poivre, sweetbreads with mushroom sauce, and sole meunière are served in a friendly, intimate dining room, which is now air-conditioned. **Known for:** French comfort food; good value prix-fixe menu; wine list. $ *Average main: €24* ⊠ *Allée de l'Ancienne Geôle, Marigot* ☎ *590/87–97–09* ⊗ *Closed Sun.*

★ Friar's Bay Beach Café

$$ | **BISTRO** | **FAMILY** | There is a sophisticated vibe at this quiet, rather elegant beach club that may make you feel as if you're on a private beach. You can rent lounge chairs and umbrellas and spend the whole day relaxing, drinking, and dining. **Known for:** beachside dining; informal atmosphere; good specials. $ *Average main: €18* ✉ *Friar's Bay Rd., Anse des Pères* ☎ *0590/49–16–87* 💳 *No credit cards* 🕙 *No dinner.*

Tropicana

$$$ | **FRENCH** | This bustling bistro at the Marina Port La Royale stays busy thanks to a varied menu, (relatively) reasonable prices, and friendly staff. Salads are superb lunch options, especially the salade Niçoise with medallions of crusted goat cheese. **Known for:** inside and outside dining; steak and seafood; crème brûlée. $ *Average main: €21* ✉ *Marina Port La Royale, Marigot* ☎ *0590/87–79–07.*

🍸 Nightlife

Kali's Beach Bar

BARS/PUBS | This happening spot has featured live music late into the night since the late 1980s. On the night of the full moon and on every Friday night, the beach bonfire and late-night party here is the place to be, but it's a great place to hang out all day long on chaises you can rent for the day. Be sure to ask Kali for some tastes of his homemade fruit-infused rum. ✉ *Anse des Pères* ☎ *690/49–06–81.*

🛍 Shopping

Longchamp

SHOES/LUGGAGE/LEATHER GOODS | This is the local outpost for the chic French leather-goods company, with an especially good selection of the Pliage line of foldable, durable, coated-zipper totes with leather handles. ✉ *1 rue du Général de Gaulle, Marigot* ☎ *0590/87–92–76* ⊕ *www.longchamp.com* 🕙 *Closed Sun.*

Max Mara

CLOTHING | These beautifully made, tailored women's clothes have an elegant attitude. ✉ *33 rue du Kennedy, Marigot* ☎ *0590/52–99–75* 🕙 *Closed Sun.*

Minguet Art Gallery

ART GALLERIES | On Rambaud Hill between Marigot and Grand Case, this gallery is managed by the daughter of the late artist Alexandre Minguet. It carries original paintings, lithographs,

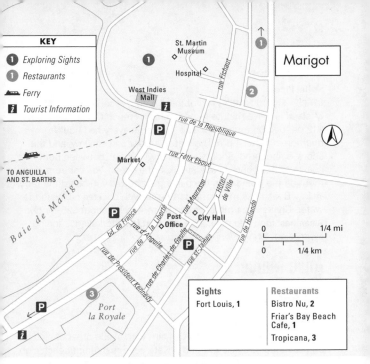

posters, and postcards depicting island flora and landscapes by Minguet and is a popular tourist attraction on the island. Call before visiting to be sure they're open. ⊠ *Rambaud* ☎ *0590/87–76–06.*

120% Lino

CLOTHING | This store has nicely made classy shirts and pants made of pure linen in pastel tones. ⊠ *A21 Marina Port La Royale, Marigot* ☎ *590/87–25–43* ⊕ *www.120percento.com.*

French Cul de Sac

North of Orient Bay Beach, the French colonial mansion of St. Martin's mayor is nestled in the hills. Little red-roof houses look like open umbrellas tumbling down the green hillside. The area is peaceful and good for hiking. From the beach here, shuttle boats make the five-minute trip to Ilet Pinel, an uninhabited island that's fine for picnicking, snorkeling, sunning, and swimming. There are full-service restaurants and beach clubs there, so just pack the sunscreen and head over.

🏖 Beaches

★ Îlet Pinel

BEACH—SIGHT | FAMILY | A protected nature reserve, this kid-friendly island is a five-minute ferry ride from French Cul de Sac (about $12 per person round-trip). The ferry runs every half hour from midmorning until 4 pm. The water is clear and shallow, and the shore is sheltered. Snorkelers can swim a trail between both coasts of this pencil-shape speck in the ocean. You can rent equipment on the island or in the parking lot before you board the ferry. Yellow Beach has more of a party vibe with cocktail tables in the water. Chairs and umbrellas can be rented for about $25 for two. **Amenities:** food and drink; parking. **Best for:** snorkeling; sunning; swimming. ⊠ *Ilet Pinel.*

Anse Marcel

🍽 Restaurants

★ Anse Marcel Beach

$$$ | MODERN FRENCH | Beachside calm with a side order of chic is on the menu at this lovely and private cove restaurant/beach club, good for a beach day, a sunset cocktail, and great swimming. You can dine and lounge all day, either in the restaurant or on the beach. **Known for:** seafood, especially the local catch; modern, pleasant atmosphere; beachfront dining. ⑤ *Average main: €24* ⊠ *Anse Marcel Beach, Anse Marcel* ☎ *0690/26–38–50* ⊕ *www.ansemarcelbeach.com.*

🛏 Hotels

★ SECRETS Hotel and Spa

$$$ | RESORT | Formerly a RIU Palace, this all-inclusive hotel was reopened as SECRETS in 2020 with 258 rooms from partial ocean view to swim-out suites, plus multiple dining options, including a poolside grill, café, and Caribbean and Asian restaurants. **Pros:** all-inclusive; activities galore; great beach and huge pool. **Cons:** remote; beach may be busy; renovations may continue through 2020. ⑤ *Rooms from: €* ⊠ *BP 581, Anse Marcel* ☎ *0590/87–67–00* ⊕ *www.secretsresorts.com/en_us/resorts/st-martin/st-martin.html* 🛏 *258 rooms* ⑩ *All-inclusive.*

Anse Marcel Beach is a great spot for swimming, dining, and lounging.

Baie Nettlé

🍴 Restaurants

⭐ La Cigale

$$$$ | FRENCH | On the edge of Baie Nettlé, this restaurant has won-derful views of the lagoon from its dining room and open-air patio, but the charm comes from the devoted attention of adorable owner Olivier, helped by his mother and brother and various cousins. The delicious food is edible sculpture: ravioli of lobster with wild mush-rooms and foie gras are poached in an intense lobster bisque, and house-smoked gravlax and salmon is garnished with a garlic cream sauce. **Known for:** artistic presentation; excellent service; convenient location near Marigot. $ *Average main: €43* ⊠ *101 Laguna Beach, Baie Nettlé* ☎ *0590/87–90–23* ⊕ *www.restaurant-lacigale.com* ⊗ *Closed Sun. and Sept. and Oct. No lunch.*

Mezza Luna

$$$ | ITALIAN | FAMILY | Though Mezza Luna's beach views are now gone due to Hurricane Irma, it's still worth coming for the excellent pizza. Their chalkboard describes all the varieties, which are many, and the pricing is very reasonable. **Known for:** variety of pizza; homemade pasta; reasonable prices. $ *Average main: €28* ⊠ *501 Nettlé Bay Beach Club, Baie Nettlé* ☎ *590–690/73–19–18.*

🛏 Hotels

★ Hotel Mercure St. Martin and Marina

$ | RESORT | FAMILY | Renovated after Hurricane Irma, this modern option with an arty vibe by a quiet beach is centrally located in Baie Nettlé, just west of Marigot, the French capital. **Pros:** good location; pet- and family-friendly; great spa and activities. **Cons:** lagoon-side beach isn't on the ocean (this is across the street); ground-floor rooms may be noisy and have no view; construction may create minimal noise. 🜚 *Rooms from: €228* ✉ *Baie Nettlé* ☎ *0590/87–54–54* ⊕ *www.mercure.com* ⇥ *170 rooms* ⫶◯⫶ *Breakfast.*

Grand Case

Grand Case was hit especially hard by Hurricane Irma in 2017 and, as a consequence of challenging government regulations, has been slower than other parts of the island to recover. Once called "The Culinary Capital of the Caribbean" since the '90s, this French side town is making efforts to rebound. It's an easy 10-minute drive from either Orient Bay or Marigot, stretching along a narrow beach overlooking Anguilla. At lunchtime, or with kids, head to the casual *lolos* (open-air grills) and feet-in-the-sand beach bars. At night, stroll the strip and preview the sophisticated offerings on the menus posted outside before you settle in for a long and sumptuous meal (reservations are required for some of the top restaurants, and they're essential in winter, high season).

🌀 Beaches

Baie de Grand Case

BEACH—SIGHT | FAMILY | Along this skinny stripe of a beach bordering the culinary village of Grand Case, the old-style gingerbread architecture sometimes peeps out between the bustling restaurants and boutiques. The sea is usually quite calm, and there are tons of fun lunch options from bistros to beachside grills (called *lolos*). Several of the restaurants rent chairs and umbrellas; some include their use for lunch patrons. In between there is a bit of shopping—for beach necessities but also for the same kinds of handicrafts found in the Marigot market. **Amenities:** food and drink; toilets. **Best for:** swimming; walking. ✉ *Grand Case.*

🍴 Restaurants

★ Bacchus

$$ | **FRENCH** | The best wine importer in the Caribbean, Benjamin Laurent, and his wife Magali have built a lively, immaculate, deliciously air-conditioned wine cellar that also just so happens to serve outstanding starters, salads, and main courses made from top ingredients brought in from France. The place is well worth the effort it may take to find it, in the Hope Estate commercial area south of the main road (Deviation de Grand Case). **Known for:** great sandwiches and wine; French pastries; strong coffee. $ *Average main: €20* ⊠ *18–19 Hope Estate, Grand Case Rd., Grand Case* ☏ *0590/87–15–70* ☉ *Closed Sun. No dinner.*

★ Cynthia's Talk of the Town

$$ | **CARIBBEAN** | **FAMILY** | One of the half-dozen lolos in the middle of town on the water side, Cynthia's (better known simply as "Talk of the Town") is a fun, relatively cheap, and iconic St. Martin meal. With plastic utensils and paper plates, it couldn't be more informal, and the menu includes everything from succulent grilled ribs to stewed conch, fresh snapper, and grilled lobster. **Known for:** lobster; succulent ribs; low pricing and big portions. $ *Average main: €14* ⊠ *Bd. de Grand Case, Grand Case* ☏ *0590/35–67–84* ▭ *No credit cards.*

L'Auberge Gourmande

$$$ | **FRENCH** | With a formal, French-provincial dining room framed by elegant arches, L'Auberge Gourmande is in one of the island's oldest Creole houses. On the walls are small etchings that look like they're 100 years old, but they're actually contemporary works by renowned island impressionist Sir Roland Richardson. **Known for:** high-end traditional dining; Dover sole in almond butter; creative desserts. $ *Average main: €27* ⊠ *89 bd. de Grand Case, Grand Case* ☏ *0590/87–73–37* ⊕ *www.laubergegourmande.com* ☉ *Closed Sept. No lunch.*

Le Cottage

$$$ | **FRENCH** | French cuisine is prepared with a light touch and presented with flair at Le Cottage, where a lively community gathers on the street-front porch. There have been themed "tasting" plates with interesting variations on an ingredient. **Known for:** loyal following; convenient location on Blvd. de Grand Case; coveted porch seating that should be reserved in advance. $ *Average main: €29* ⊠ *97 bd. de Grand Case, Grand Case* ☏ *0590/690–622–686* ⊕ *www.lecottagesxm.com* ☉ *No lunch.*

★ Rainbow Cafe & Beach Bar

$$$ | INTERNATIONAL | FAMILY | Bringing style, wit, and a bit of panache to the beach bar genre, Rainbow delivers a memorable breakfast, lunch, and dinner on their beachfront deck. Choose a front-row seat (or lounge chair) on Grand Case beach and choose from an eclectic menu, which includes vegetarian and vegan selections, offers steak, grilled fish, raw fish, and lobster, too. **Known for:** SXM's most upscale beach bar; a spectrum of experiences for all palate cravings; people-watching. $ *Average main: €26* ⊠ *176 bd. de Grand Case, Grand Case* ☎ *590/690–888–444* ⊕ *www.rainbowcafe.fr* ☉ *Closed Mon.* ▭ *No credit cards.*

Spiga

$$$ | ITALIAN | In a beautifully restored Creole house, exceptional cuisine fuses Italian and occasionally some Caribbean ingredients and cooking techniques. Follow one of the ample appetizers with an excellent pasta, fresh fish, or meat dish, such as the pesto-crusted rack of lamb. **Known for:** creative Italian cuisine; porch dining; outstanding desserts. $ *Average main: €29* ⊠ *4 rte. de L'Espérance, Grand Case* ☎ *0590/52–47–83* ⊕ *www.spiga-sxm.com* ☉ *Closed mid-Sept.–late Oct. and Tues. in June–mid-Sept. No lunch.*

Hotels

Bleu Emeraude

$$ | RENTAL | FAMILY | The 11 spacious apartments in this tidy complex sit right on a sliver of Grand Case Beach. **Pros:** modern and updated; walk to restaurants; attractive decor. **Cons:** neighborhood can be noisy; far from Philipsburg, the island's shopping capital; can be an hour or more from the airport on busy days. $ *Rooms from: €360* ⊠ *240 bd. de Grand Case, Grand Case* ☎ *0590/87–27–71* ⊕ *www.bleuemeraude.com* ⇆ *11 units* ⦿ *Free Breakfast.*

★ Grand Case Beach Club

$$ | RESORT | FAMILY | Easily the finest beach resort in Grand Case (and better than ever after post-Hurricane Irma renovations), "GCBC" has a friendly staff and incredible sunset views. **Pros:** reasonably priced for what you get; completely renovated post-Irma; walking distance to fine-dining restaurants. **Cons:** small beach; some ongoing minor renovations; need a car to explore. $ *Rooms from: €366* ⊠ *21 rue de la Petite Plage, at East / North end of bd. de Grand Case, Grand Case* ☎ *0590/87–51–87, 800/344–3016 in U.S.* ⊕ *www.grandcasebeachclub.com* ⇆ *72 apartments* ⦿ *Breakfast.*

★ Hôtel L'Esplanade

$$$ | HOTEL | FAMILY | Fans return year after year to the classy, loft-style suites in this immaculate family-owned and operated

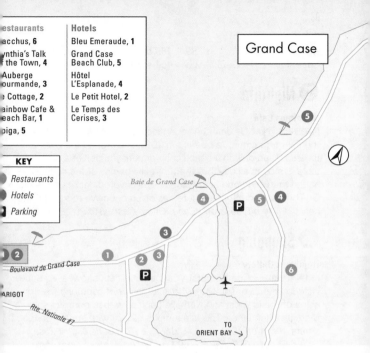

Grand Case

Restaurants
acchus, **6**
ynthia's Talk
f the Town, **4**
Auberge
ourmande, **3**
e Cottage, **2**
ainbow Cafe &
each Bar, **1**
piga, **5**

Hotels
Bleu Emeraude, **1**
Grand Case
Beach Club, **5**
Hôtel
L'Esplanade, **4**
Le Petit Hotel, **2**
Le Temps des
Cerises, **3**

KEY
Restaurants
Hotels
Parking

Baie de Grand Case

Boulevard de Grand Case

ARIGOT

Rte. Nationale #7

TO
ORIENT BAY →

boutique hotel, located on a hill overlooking Grand Case village and its harbor. **Pros:** highly attentive management; clean and beautiful; family-friendly. **Cons:** lots of stairs; not on the beach; the pool, spa, and yoga area are a bit of a walk from the rooms. $ *Rooms from: €415 ⊠ Grand Case ☎ 0590/87–06–55, 866/596–8365 in U.S. ⊕ www.lesplanade.com ➥ 24 units ⊗ No meals.*

★ Le Petit Hotel

$$$ | **HOTEL** | **FAMILY** | With some of the best restaurants in the Caribbean just steps away, this attractive beachfront boutique hotel exudes charm and has the same caring, attentive management as Hotel L'Esplanade. **Pros:** walking distance to everything in Grand Case; friendly staff; clean, bright, updated rooms. **Cons:** some stairs to climb; no pool; on-site parking is tight. $ *Rooms from: €435 ⊠ 248 bd. de Grand Case, Grand Case ☎ 0590/29–09–65 ⊕ www.lepetithotel.com ➥ 10 rooms ⊗ Free Breakfast.*

★ Le Temps des Cerises

$$ | **B&B/INN** | Named for the classic 19th-century French chanson, Le Temps des Cerises is the first hotel representing the fashion house of the same name based in Marseille and was completely rebuilt after Hurricane Irma in 2017. **Pros:** chic decor; comfortable rooms; right on the beach. **Cons:** can be a bit noisy; across the island from Princess Juliana airport; a car is necessary to see the sights. $ *Rooms from: €280* ✉ *158 bd. de Grand Case, Grand Case* ☎ *590/51–36–27* ⊕ *www.ltc-hotel.com* ↩ *9 rooms.*

🍸 Nightlife

★ Calmos Café

GATHERING PLACES | Join the young local crowd by walking through the T-shirt boutique, re-opened in 2019, and around the back to the sea. Then pull up a beach chair or park yourself at a picnic table. It's open all day, but the fun really begins at the cocktail hour, when everyone enjoys tapas. The covered deck is romantic. On Thursday and Sunday there has often been live reggae on the beach. ✉ *40 bd. de Grand Case, Grand Case* ☎ *0590/29–01–85.*

🛍 Shopping

Tropismes Gallery

ART GALLERIES | Contemporary Caribbean artists showcased here include Paul Elliot Thuleau, who is a master of capturing the sunshine of the islands, and Nathalie Lepine, whose portraits show a Modigliani influence. This is a serious gallery with some very good artists. It's open 10–1 and 5–9 daily. ✉ *107 bd. de Grand Case, Grand Case* ☎ *0690/54–62–69* ⊕ *www.tropismesgallery.com.*

Voila!!!

CLOTHING | The trendy beach attire, arty accessories, and souvenirs are fun to try on and buy here. Late hours mean you can shop before or after dinner. ✉ *101 bd. de Grand Case, Grand Case* ☎ *590/690–73–74–13* ⊕ *www.voilasxm.com.*

Orléans

North of Oyster Pond and the Étang aux Poissons (Fish Lake) is the island's oldest settlement, also known as the French Quarter. You can still see a few vibrantly painted West Indian–style homes with the original gingerbread fretwork. There are also large areas of the nature and marine preserve working to save the island's fragile ecosystem.

🍴 Restaurants

Yvette's Restaurant

$$ | **CARIBBEAN** | **FAMILY** | Follow the locals to Yvette's Kitchen, in a private house, for the island's best creole-Cajun cooking. All the St. Martin favorites are dished up in big portions at a reasonable price. **Known for:** pickled conch; hot johnnycakes; curry goat.

⑤ *Average main: €19* ✉ *Quartier d'Orléans* ✛ *Off the main road of Quartier d'Orleans, across the road from the pharmacy* ☎ *590/87–32–03* ⊗ *Closed Wed.* ▭ *No credit cards.*

Pic Paradis

Between Marigot and Grand Case, Paradise Peak (Pic Paradis), at 1,492 feet, is the island's highest point. There are two observation areas. From them, the tropical forest unfolds below, and the vistas are breathtaking. The road is quite isolated and steep, best suited to a four-wheel-drive vehicle. There continue to be some problems with crime in this area, so it might be best to go hiking with an experienced local guide, if at all; better to visit Loterie Farm, which is off the main road headed to Pic Paradis.

⊙ Sights

★ Loterie Farm
NATURE PRESERVE | FAMILY | Almost halfway up the road to Pic Paradis is a peaceful 150-acre private nature preserve, opened to the public in 1999 by American expat B. J. Welch. There are trail maps, so you can hike on your own or hire a guide. Marked trails traverse native forest with tamarind, gum, mango, and mahogany trees—the same as it was hundreds of years ago. You might well see some wild vervet monkeys, now rather common here. L'Eau Lounge is a lovely tropical garden with a chain of spring-fed pools and Jacuzzi area plus pool with lounge chairs, great music, roaming iguanas, and chic tented cabanas with a St. Barth–meets–Wet 'n' Wild atmosphere. A delicious, healthy lunch or dinner can be had at NuitLeau, and if you are brave—and over 4 feet 5 inches tall—you can try soaring over trees on one of the longest ziplines in the western hemisphere. (There is a milder version, but people love the more extreme one.) "Treehab," a wild party at the end of every month, brings the island's best DJs; and the Garden Groove Party enlivens every Saturday night in June, July, and August. It features barbecue, drinks, DJs, live music, and entertainers. A new 9-hole golf course added in 2019 promises to give the course on the Dutch side in Mullet Bay some competition. ✉ *103 rte. de Pic du Paradis, Rambaud* ☎ *0590/87–86–16* ⊕ *www.loteriefarm. com* 🎟 *Hiking €5, guide €26, zipline €40–€60.*

St. Maarten vs. St. Martin

If this is your first trip to St. Maarten/St. Martin, you're probably wondering which side will better suit your needs. That's hard to say, because in some ways the difference between the two can seem as subtle as the open boundary dividing them. But there are some major distinctions.

St. Maarten, the Dutch side, has the casinos, more nightlife, smaller price tags (thanks in part to the French side's euro), and bigger hotels. Cruise ships dock here. St. Martin, the French side, has no casinos, less nightlife, and hotels that are smaller and more intimate. Many have kitchenettes, and most include breakfast. If you're looking for fine dining, that used to be concentrated in Grand Case on the French side, but now there's extraordinary dining from one end of the island to the other; look especially now at both Porto Cupecoy and Simpson Bay on the Dutch side.

Baie Orientale

Even though Hurricane Irma destroyed nearly every business on Orient Beach in 2017, they're practically all back now, and the beach is as vibrant as ever (wider, even, with more sand to enjoy now than in years). Many consider this the island's most beautiful beach, with 2 miles (3 km) of champagne sand, underwater marine reserve, a variety of water sports, and re-emerging beach clubs and hotels. At its southern end, "naturists" enjoy the Club Orient area's clothing-optional policy, limited by regulation to that portion of the beach only. (Topless sunbathing is allowed on the entire beach.) Naturally, cameras are forbidden and may be confiscated. Plan to spend the day at one of the clubs; each bar has different color umbrellas, and most boast excellent restaurants and lively bars. The beach starts to empty like clockwork daily around 4 pm. To get here from Marigot, take the main road north past Grand Case, past the French side Aéroport de L'Espérance, and watch for the left turn.

🌀 Beaches

★ Baie Orientale (*Orient Bay*)
BEACH—SIGHT | FAMILY | Even though Hurricane Irma destroyed nearly every business on Orient Beach in 2017, they're practically all back now, and the beach is as vibrant as ever (wider even, with more sand to enjoy now than in years). Many consider this the island's most beautiful beach, with 2 miles (3 km) of champagne sand, underwater

marine reserve, a variety of water sports, and re-emerging beach clubs and hotels. At its southern end, "naturists" enjoy the Club Orient area's clothing-optional policy, limited by regulation to that portion of the beach only. (Topless sunbathing is allowed on the entire beach.) Naturally, cameras are forbidden and may be confiscated. Plan to spend the day at one of the clubs; each bar has different color umbrellas, and most boast excellent restaurants and lively bars. You can have an open-air massage, try any sea toy you fancy, and stay until late afternoon, though the beach starts to empty like clockwork daily around 4 p.m. To get here from Marigot, take the main road north past Grand Case, past the French side Aéroport de L'Espérance, and watch for the left turn. **Amenities:** food and drink; parking; toilets; water sports. **Best for:** nudists; partiers; swimming; walking; windsurfing. ⊠ *Baie Orientale.*

Club Orient Resort

Club Orient, the only naturist resort on Orient Beach, has vowed to rebuild and reopen after being destroyed by Hurricane Irma in 2017, but at the time of this writing the Club remained closed with no sign of a quick return. The nude beach and "Perch Lite" snack bar, however, are open, drawing hundreds of visitors daily.

🍽 Restaurants

★ L'Astrolabe

$$$ | FRENCH | L'Astrolabe gets raves for its modern interpretations of classic French cuisine served around the pool at this cozy, relaxed restaurant in the Esmeralda Resort. Menu highlights include lobster and cognac bisque, home-smoked yellowfin tuna, foie gras over brioche, Trigger fish tempura, black Angus beef, boneless lamb shoulder, and Madagascar fresh vanilla crème brûlée. **Known for:** classic French dining, by the pool; foie gras tasting; Dover sole meunière. 🅢 *Average main: €26* ⊠ *Esmeralda Resort, Baie Orientale* ☎ *0590/87–11–20* ⊕ *www.astrolabe-sxm.com* 𝄐 *No lunch. No dinner Wed.*

La Table d'Antoine

$$$ | FRENCH | FAMILY | Settle in here for an evening of attentive, friendly service and hearty French bistro-style country food with a side dish of lively people-watching. The varied menu features slightly unfamiliar dishes that are worth a try: take the plunge, you will not be disappointed. **Known for:** tuna tataki; shrimp risotto; duck with figs. 🅢 *Average main: €25* ⊠ *Pl. de la Baie Orientale,*

Whether you're on St. Maarten or St. Martin, the sunsets are unforgettable.

Baie Orientale ☎ *0590/52–97–57* ⊕ *www.latabledantoinesxm.com* ⊙ *Closed Tues. Closed Mon. in low season.*

Hotels

Esmeralda Resort

$$ | RESORT | FAMILY | Now reopened after Irma, Esmeralda has traditional Caribbean-style, kitchen-equipped villas that can be configured to meet guests' needs, have their own pool, and offer the fun of Orient Beach a short walk away. **Pros:** beachfront location; private pools; plenty of activities. **Cons:** need a car to get around; iffy Wi-Fi service; surrounding area continues to rebuild after Irma. $ *Rooms from: €341* ✉ *Baie Orientale* ☎ *0590/87–36–36* ⊕ *www.esmeralda-resort.com* ⊙ *Closed Sept. and Oct.* ⇆ *65 rooms* ⦿⦿ *Breakfast.*

★ Hotel La Plantation

$ | HOTEL | FAMILY | Perched high above Baie Orientale, this fully restored-post-Irma colonial-style hotel is a charmer; French doors open to a wraparound verandah with an expansive view of the bay. **Pros:** relaxing atmosphere; eye-popping views; lots of area restaurants. **Cons:** small pool; beach is a 10-minute walk away; car or taxi needed to get to other major tourist areas. $ *Rooms from: €167* ✉ *C5 Parc de La Baie Orientale, Baie Orientale* ☎ *0590/29–58–00* ⊕ *www.la-plantation.com* ⊙ *Normally closed Sept.–mid-Oct.* ⇆ *51 rooms* ⦿⦿ *Breakfast.*

★ La Playa Orient Bay

$$$ | RESORT | You can't miss the multistory candy-colored villas right on beautiful Orient Beach, beautifully renovated after Hurricane Irma. **Pros:** spacious rooms; funky, friendly atmosphere; attractive beach location. **Cons:** minimum length stay may be required in high season; car needed to visit other tourist areas; daily except Sunday getting to the airport can take up to an hour (traffic). $ *Rooms from: $439* ⊠ *La Playa Orient Bay, 116 Parc de la Baie Orientale, Baie Orientale* 590/87–42–08 ⊕ *www.laplaya-orientbay.com* 56 rooms ⦿ *Free Breakfast.*

★ Palm Court at Orient Beach Hotel

$ | HOTEL | The romantic beachfront units of this *hôtel de charme* are steps from the fun of Orient Beach yet private, quiet, and stylish. **Pros:** big rooms; romantic decor; nice garden. **Cons:** across from, but not on, the beach; car required to get to distant key tourist areas; daily except Sunday, driving in traffic to the airport can take an hour. $ *Rooms from: €231* ⊠ *Parc de la Baie Orientale, Baie Orientale* 800/480–8555, 590/87–41–94 ⊕ *palmcourt-hotel.com* ⊗ *Closed Sept.* 24 rooms ⦿ *Breakfast.*

Sol e Luna Guesthouse

$$ | B&B/INN | Independent couples who don't want a big resort love the six comfortable suites in this hillside guesthouse overlooking a pretty pool, a salt pond, and on to Orient Bay. Recently renovated and decorated in a modern Italian style with tropical details, the attractive and spacious suites have Italian marble baths, compact kitchenettes, and dining patios. **Pros:** spacious suites; good location for exploring; excellent on-site restaurant. **Cons:** not a full-service hotel; need a car; quite a few steps to climb around the property. $ *Rooms from: €304* ⊠ *61 Mont Vernon, Baie Orientale* 590/29–08–56 ⊕ *www.solelunarestaurant.com* ⊗ *Closed Sept.* 6 suites.

Baie Longue

Though it extends over the French Lowlands, from the cliff at La Samanna to La Pointe des Canniers, the island's longest beach has no facilities or vendors. It's a great place for a romantic walk, but be aware that getting here isn't as easy as it once was since you must now pass through Lowlands security. Note that the beach faces westward and can get very hot; there's no shade from trees, either. This beach is on the leeward, less breezy side of the island. To get here, take National Road 7 south of Marigot. Baie Longue Road is the first entrance to the beach. It's worth a splurge for lunch or a sunset cocktail at the elegant La Samanna.

Belmond La Samanna is known for its great beach and spa.

🛏️ Hotels

⭐ Belmond La Samanna

$$$$ | **RESORT** | **FAMILY** | A complete overhaul after Hurricane Irma has helped keep La Samanna, bordered by a pristine, white-sand beach, the island's top luxury resort. **Pros:** chic decor; great beach and spa; beach cabanas, convenient location. **Cons:** expensive; small pools; car required to get to off-site restaurants and shopping. ⑤ *Rooms from: €905* ✉ *Baie Longue* ☎ *0590/87–64–00, 800/854–2252 in U.S.* ⊕ *www.belmond.com/la-samanna-st-martin* ☉ *Usually closed Sept. and Oct.* 🛏️ *81 rooms* ❝❞ *Breakfast.*

👜 Shopping

⭐ La Samanna Spa

FITNESS/HEALTH CLUBS | You don't have to be a guest at the hotel to enjoy a treatment or a day package at this heavenly retreat, easily one of the top spas on the island. In a lovely tropical garden setting, immaculate treatment rooms feature walled gardens with private outdoor showers. There are dozens of therapies for body, face, hair, and spirit on the spa menu; any can be customized to your desires or sensitivities. Open daily 10–7. ✉ *Belmond La Samanna, Baie Longue* ☎ *0590/87–65–69* ⊕ *www.belmond.com/la-samanna-st-martin.*

ST. BARTHÉLEMY

Updated by
Jeff Berger

👁 Sights   🍴 Restaurants   🛏 Hotels   🛍 Shopping   🍸 Nightlife

★★★★☆   ★★★★★   ★★★★★   ★★★★★   ★★★★★

WELCOME TO ST. BARTHÉLEMY

TOP REASONS TO GO

★ **The Scene:** The island is active, sexy, hedonistic, and hip, and the human scenery is as beautiful as the sparkling-blue sea vistas.

★ **Super Style:** St. Barth continues to change and evolve, becoming ever more chic.

★ **Great Dining:** New restaurants tempt gourmets and gourmands.

★ **Shopping Galore:** If you're a shopper, you'll find bliss stalking the latest in French clothes and accessories with prices up to 30% less than in the States.

★ **Getting Out on the Water:** Windsurfing, kitesurfing, and other water sports make going to the beach more than just a lounging experience.

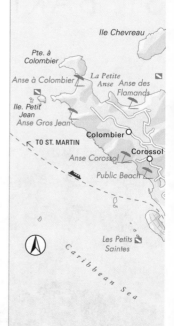

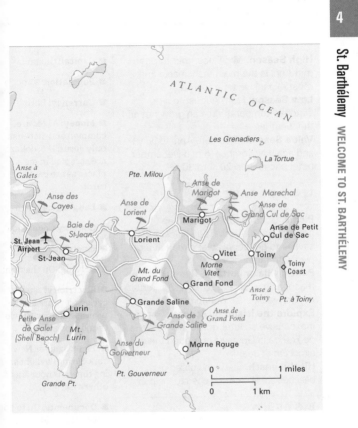

ISLAND SNAPSHOT

WHEN TO GO

High Season: Mid-December through mid-April is the most fashionable and most expensive time to visit.
Low Season: From August to late October, temperatures can grow hot and the weather.
Value Season: From late April to July and again November to mid-December, hotel prices drop 20% to 30%

WAYS TO SAVE

Picnic. Good food requires deep pockets on St. Barth. The easiest way to save is to get supplies at a market and picnic on the beach.
Rent a villa or cottage. There are some reasonable villas and cottages for rent by the week, even during high season.
Explore the island by scooter. Rent an inexpensive scooter or moped from rue de France in Gustavia or around the airport in St-Jean.
Hit the beach. St. Barth's dozen-plus beaches are all free and open to the public.

BIG EVENTS

January: The St. Barth Music Festival showcases a wide variety of musical and dance performances usually held the second and third weeks of the month.
⊕ www.stbartsmusicfestival.org

April: St. Barth Festival of Caribbean Cinema celebrates Caribbean-made documentaries and feature films.
⊕ www.stbarthff.org

October: The *Taste of St. Barth* is an international gourmet food festival that brings renowned chefs to the island.

AT A GLANCE

■ **Capital:** Gustavia

■ **Population:** 8,400

■ **Currency:** Euro

■ **Money:** ATMs are common and dispense only euros; U.S. dollars are accepted in most places as are credit cards.

■ **Language:** French

■ **Country Code:** 590

■ **Emergencies:** 18

■ **Driving:** On the right

■ **Electricity:** 230v/60 cycles; plugs are European standard with two round prongs

■ **Time:** Same as New York during daylight saving time; one hour ahead otherwise

■ **Documents:** Up to 90 days with valid passport

■ **Mobile Phones:** GSM (900 and 1800 bands)

■ **Major Mobile Companies:** Digicel, Orange, CHIPPIE, Dauphin Telecom

■ **St. Barths Online:** ⊕ www.st-barths.com

■ **Office du Tourisme:** ⊕ www.saintbarth-tourisme.com

St. Barthélemy blends the respective essences of the Caribbean, France, and *Architectural Digest* in perfect proportions. A sophisticated but unstudied approach to relaxation and respite prevails: you can spend the day on a beach, try on the latest French fashions, catch a gallery exhibition, and watch the sunset while nibbling tapas over Gustavia Harbor, then choose from nearly 100 excellent restaurants for an elegant or easy evening meal. You can putter around the island, scuba dive, windsurf on a quiet cove, or just admire the lovely views.

A mere 8 square miles (21 square km), St. Barth is a hilly island, with many sheltered inlets and picturesque, quiet beaches. The town of Gustavia wraps itself around a modern harbor lined with everything from size-matters megayachts to rustic fishing boats to sailboats of all descriptions. Red-roof villas dot the hillsides, and glass-front shops line the streets. Beach surf runs the gamut from kiddie-pool calm to serious-surfer dangerous, beaches from deserted to packed. The cuisine is tops in the Caribbean, and almost everything is tidy, stylish, and up-to-date. French *savoir vivre* prevails.

Christopher Columbus came to the island—called "Ouanalao" by its native Caribs—in 1493; he named it for his brother Bartolomé. The first French colonists arrived in 1648, drawn by its location on the West Indian Trade Route, but they were wiped out by the Caribs, who dominated the area. Another small group from Normandy and Brittany arrived in 1694. This time the settlers prospered—with the help of French buccaneers, who took advantage of the island's strategic location and protected harbor. In 1784 the French traded the island to King Gustav III of Sweden in exchange for port rights in Göteborg. The king dubbed the capital Gustavia, laid out and paved streets, built three forts, and turned the community into a prosperous free port. The island thrived as a shipping and commercial center until the 19th century, when earthquakes, fires, and hurricanes brought financial ruin. Many residents fled to newer lands of opportunity, and Oscar II of Sweden returned the island to France. After briefly considering selling it to America, the French took possession of St. Barthélemy again on August 10, 1877.

Today the island is a free port, and in 2007 it became a Collectivité, a French-administered overseas territory. Arid, hilly, and rocky, St. Barth was unsuited to sugar production and thus never developed an extensive slave base. Some of the residents are descendants of the tough Norman and Breton settlers of three centuries ago, but you are more likely to encounter attractive French twenty- and thirtysomethings from Normandy and Provence, who are friendly, English-speaking, and here for the sunny lifestyle.

Planning

Getting Here and Around

AIR TRAVEL

Because of its tiny, hillside runway, there are no direct major-airline flights to St. Barth. Most North Americans fly first into St. Maarten's Princess Juliana International SXM Airport, from which the island is a quick 12 minutes by air. Winair has frequent flights from St. Maarten every day. Through Winair's affiliation with major airlines, you can check your luggage from your home airport through to St. Barth under certain circumstances. Tradewind Aviation has regularly scheduled service from San Juan and also does VIP charters. Anguilla Air Services and St. Barth Commuter have scheduled flights and also do charters. *Leave ample time between your scheduled flight and your connection in St. Maarten: 90 minutes is the minimum recommended* (and be aware that luggage frequently doesn't make the trip; your hotel or villa-rental company may be able to send someone to retrieve it). It's a good idea to pack a change of clothes, required medicines, and a bathing suit in your carry-on—or better yet, pack very light and don't check baggage at all.

AIRPORTS Gustaf III Airport (SBH). ⊠ *St. Jean Rd., St-Jean* ☎ *0590/27–75–81.*

AIRLINES St. Barth Commuter. ☎ *0590/27–54–54* ⊕ *www.stbarth-commuter.com.* **Tradewind Aviation.** ☎ *203/267–3305* ⊕ *www.fly-tradewind.com.* **Trans Anguilla Airways.** ☎ *264/498–5922* ⊕ *www.*

transanguilla.com. **Winair.**
☎ *0590/27–61–01, 866/466–0410* ⊕ *www.fly-winair.com.*

BOAT AND FERRY TRAVEL
St. Barth can be reached via ferry service from St. Maarten/ St. Martin to Quai de la République in Gustavia. Voyager offers several daily round-trips for about $110 per person from Marigot. Great Bay Express has multiple round-trips daily from the Dutch side of St. Maarten for roughly €90 if reserved in advance, €95 for same-day tickets, and €56 each way for a same-day round-trip. Private boat charters are also available, but they are very expensive; Master Ski Pilou offers transfers from St. Maarten.

> ### Backup Ferry ◉
>
> Even if you are flying to St. Barth, it's a good idea to keep the numbers and schedules for the ferry companies handy in case your flight is delayed. If you are planning to spend time in St. Maarten before traveling on to St. Barth, the ferry may be lower in cost, and you can leave from Marigot or Philipsburg.

CONTACTS Great Bay Express. ✉ *Quai Gustavia, Gustavia* ☎ *721/520–5015* ⊕ *www.greatbayferry.com.* **Master Ski Pilou.** ☎ *0590/27–91–79* ⊕ *www.masterski-pilou.com.* **Voyager.** ☎ *0590/87–10–68* ⊕ *www.voy12.com.*

CAR TRAVEL
Roads are sometimes unmarked, so get a map and look for signs, nailed to posts at all crossroads, pointing to a destination. Roads are narrow and sometimes very steep, but have been improved; even so, check the brakes and low gears before driving away from the rental office. Maximum speed is 30 mph (50 kph). Driving is on the right, as in the United States and Europe. Parking is an additional challenge. There are two gas stations on the island, one near the airport and one in Lorient. They aren't open after 5 pm or on Sunday, and pumps at the station near the airport now accept chip-and-pin credit cards. Considering the short distances, a full tank should last most of a week. ■ TIP→ **Ask your car rental company about Blue Parking Tags, which give you 1½ hours of parking for about €30. They're worth every penny.**

Car Rentals: You must have a valid driver's license and be 25 or older to rent, and in high season there may be a three-day minimum. During peak periods, such as Christmas week and February, arrange for your car rental ahead of time. Rental agencies operate out of Gustaf III Airport; some will bring your car to your hotel. Alternately, when you make your hotel reservation, ask if the hotel has its own cars available to rent; some hotels provide 24-hour emergency road service—something most rental companies don't. Expect to pay at least $55 per day, and note the company will usually hold about $500 until the car is returned. ■ TIP→ **For a green alternative, consider renting an electric car. They're available for about $85 per day.**

CONTACTS Avis. ☎ *0590/27–66–30* ⊕ *www.avis-sbh.com.* **Budget.** ☎ *0590/27–66–30* ⊕ *www.st-barths.com/budget.* **Cool Rental.** ☎ *0590/27–52–58* ⊕ *www.cool-rental.com.* **Europcar.** ☎ *0590/29–41–86* ⊕ *www.europcar-stbarth.com.* **Gumbs.** ☎ *0590/27–75–32* ⊕ *www.gumbs-car-rental.com.* **Hertz.** ☎ *0590/52–34–03* ⊕ *www.hertzstbarth.com.* **Turbé.** ☎ *0590/27–71–42* ⊕ *www.turbe-car-rental.com.*

MOPED, SCOOTER, AND BIKE TRAVEL

Several companies rent motorbikes, scooters, mopeds, ATVs, and mountain bikes. Motorbikes go for about $30 per day and require a $100 deposit. ATV rental starts at $40 per day. Helmets are required. Scooter and motorbike rental places are mostly along rue de France in Gustavia and around the airport in St-Jean. If you have not driven an ATV or "quad" before, St. Barth may not be the best place to try it out. The roads, though not jammed with traffic, are quite narrow, and navigating the hilly terrain can be quite a challenge.

CONTACTS Barthloc Rental. ✉ *Rue de France, Gustavia* ☎ *0590/27–52–81* ⊕ *www.barthloc.com.* **Chez Béranger.** ✉ *21 rue du général de Gaulle, Gustavia* ☎ *0590/27–89–00* ⊕ *www.beranger-rental.com.*

TAXI TRAVEL

Taxis are expensive and not particularly easy to arrange, especially in the evening. There's a taxi station at the airport and another at the ferry dock in Gustavia; from elsewhere you must contact a dispatcher in Gustavia or St-Jean. Fares are regulated by the Collectivity, and drivers accept both dollars and euros. If you go out to dinner by taxi, let the restaurant know if you will need a taxi at the end of the meal, and they will call one for you.

CONTACTS Taxis. ☎ *0590/52–40–40, 0590/27–75–81.* **Taxi Prestige.** ☎ *0590/27–70–57.*

Sights

With practice, negotiating St. Barth's narrow, steep roads soon becomes fun. Infrastructure upgrades and small, responsive rental cars have improved driving. Free maps are everywhere, and roads are smooth and well marked. The tourist office has annotated maps with walking tours that highlight sights of interest.

Beaches

There is a beach in St. Barth to suit every taste. Wild surf, complete privacy in nature, a dreamy white-sand strand, and a spot at a chic beach club close to shopping and restaurants—they're all within a 20-minute drive.

There are many *anses* (coves) and nearly 20 *plages* (beaches) scattered around the island, each with a distinct personality; all are open to the public, even if they front a tony resort. Because of the number of beaches, even in high season you can find a nearly empty one, despite St. Barth's tiny size. That's not to say that all beaches are equally good or even equally suitable for swimming, but each has something to offer. Unless you are having lunch at a beachfront restaurant with lounging areas set aside for patrons, you should bring an umbrella, beach mat, and drinking water (all of which are easily obtainable all over the island). Topless sunbathing is common, but nudism is *supposedly* forbidden—although both Grande Saline and Gouverneur are de facto nude beaches, albeit less than in the past. Shade is scarce.

Restaurants

Dining on St. Barth compares favorably to almost anywhere in the world. Varied and exquisite cuisine, a French flair in the decor, sensational wine, and attentive service make for a wonderful epicurean experience in almost any of the more than 80 restaurants. On most menus, freshly caught local seafood mingles on the plate with top-quality provisions that arrive regularly from Paris. Interesting selections on the Cartes de Vins are no surprise, but don't miss the sophisticated cocktails whipped up by island bartenders. They are worlds away from cliché Caribbean rum punches with paper umbrellas. The signature drink of St. Barth is called "'ti punch," a rum concoction similar to a Brazilian caipirinha. It's also fun to sit at a bar and ask the attractive bartender for his or her own signature cocktail.

Most restaurants offer a chalkboard of daily specials, usually a good bet. But even the pickiest eaters will find something on every menu. Some level of compliance will be paid to dietary restrictions, especially if explained in French; just be aware that French people generally let the chef work his or her magic. Vegetarians will find many options on every menu. Expect meals to be costly, but you can dine superbly and somewhat economically if you limit pricey cocktails, watch wine selections, share appetizers or desserts, and pick up snacks and picnics from one of the well-stocked markets. Or you can follow the locals to small *crêperies,* cafés, sandwich shops, and pizzerias in the main shopping areas. *Ti creux* means "snack" or "small bite."

Lavish publications feature restaurant menus and contacts. Ask at your hotel or look on the racks at the airport. Reservations are strongly recommended and, in high season, essential. Lots of restaurants now accept reservations on their website or by email. Check social media. Except during the Christmas–New Year's season it's not usually necessary to book far in advance. A day's—or even a few hours'—notice is usually sufficient. At the end of the meal, as in France, you must request the bill. Until you do, you can feel free to linger at the table and enjoy the complimentary vanilla rum that's likely to appear.

Check restaurant bills carefully. A *service compris* (service charge) is always added by law, but you should leave the server 5% to 10% extra in cash. You'll usually come out ahead if you charge restaurant meals on a credit card in euros instead of paying with American currency, as your credit card might offer a better exchange rate than the restaurant (unless your credit card adds a conversion surcharge). Many restaurants serve locally caught *langouste* (lobster); priced by weight. It's usually the most expensive item on a menu and, depending on its size and the restaurant, will range in price from $40 to $60 or more. *In menu prices below, lobster has been left out of the range.*

What to Wear: A bathing suit and gauzy top or shift is acceptable at beachside lunch spots, but not really in Gustavia. Jackets are never required and are rarely worn by men, but most people do dress fashionably for dinner. St. Barth is for fashionistas; women wear whatever is hip, current, and sexy. You can't go wrong in a tank dress or a sexy top with white jeans, high sandals, and flashy accessories. The sky is the limit for high fashion at nightclubs and lounges in high season, when you might (correctly) think everyone in sight is a model. Leave some space in your suitcase; you can buy the perfect outfit here on the island. Nice shorts (not beachy ones) at the dinner table may label a man *Américain,* but many locals have adopted the habit and nobody cares much. Wear them with a pastel shirt to really fit in (never tucked in). Pack a light sweater or shawl for the occasional breezy night.

Hotels and Resorts

There's no denying that hotel rooms and villas on St. Barth carry high prices. You're paying primarily for the privilege of staying on the island, and even at $800 a night the bedrooms tend to be small. Still, if you're flexible—in terms of timing and in your choice of lodgings—you can enjoy a holiday in St. Barth and still afford to send the kids to college.

The most expensive season falls during the holidays (mid-December to early January), when hotels are booked far in advance, may require a 10- or 14-day stay, and can be double the high-season rates. A 5% government tourism tax on room prices (excluding breakfast) is in effect; be sure to ask if it is included in your room rate or added on.

When it comes to booking a hotel on St. Barth, the reservation manager can be your best ally. Rooms within a property can vary greatly. It's well worth the price of a phone call or the time invested in emails to make a personal connection, which can lead to a room that meets your needs or preferences. Details of accessibility, views, recent redecorating, meal options, and special package rates are topics open for discussion. Quoted hotel rates are per room, not per person, and include service charges and often airport transfers. Bargain rates found on Internet booking sites can sometimes yield unpleasant surprises in terms of the actual room you get. Consider contacting the hotel and mentioning the rate you found. Often they will match it, and you'll end up with a better room.

Small luxury hotels: The largest hotel on the island has about 70 rooms, but the majority are stratospherically expensive.

Villas: About half the accommodations on St. Barth are in private villas.

Hotel reviews have been shortened. For full information, visit Fodors.com.

What It Costs in Euros			
$	$$	$$$	$$$$
RESTAURANTS			
under €12	€12–€20	€21–€30	over €30
HOTELS			
under €275	€275–€375	€376–€475	over €475

On St. Barth the term *villa* describes anything from a small cottage to a luxurious, modern estate. Today almost half of St. Barth's accommodations are in villas, a great option, especially if traveling with friends or family. Even more advantageous to Americans, villa rates are usually quoted in dollars, thus bypassing unfavorable euro fluctuations. Most villas have a small private swimming pool and maid service daily except Sunday. They are well furnished with linens, kitchen utensils, and such electronic necessities as smart-phone docks, TV, and Internet. Weekly in-season rates range from $1,400+ to "oh-my-gosh." Most villa-rental companies are based in the United States and have extensive websites that enable you to see pictures or panoramic videos of the place you're considering; their local offices oversee maintenance and housekeeping and provide concierge services. Just be aware that there are few beachfront villas, so if you have your heart set on "toes in the sand" and a cute waiter delivering your Kir Royale, stick with the hotels or villas operated by hotel properties.

★ Eden Rock Villa Rental

Eden Rock Villa Rental manages 80 super-luxe villas and cottages. Provided with each are butlers, chefs, and concierge services, giving you the privacy of a villa but the service of a luxury hotel. Prices are per night and range from several hundreds dollars to several thousand, but the pricier villas have more bedrooms enabling visitors to vacation with friends and share the cost. ☎ *0590/27–14–94* ⊕ *www.edenrockvillarental.com*.

Marla

This local St. Barth villa-rental company represents more than 100 villas, many of which are not listed with other companies. ✉ *18 rue du Roi Oscar II, Gustavia* ☎ *0590/27–62–02* ⊕ *www.marlavillas.com*.

St. Barth Properties, Inc.

Owned by American Peg Walsh, a regular on St. Barth since 1986, this company represents more than 120 properties. The excellent website offers virtual tours of most of the villas and even details on availability. ✉ *Gustavia* ☎ *508/528–7727, 800/421–3396* ⊕ *www.stbarth.com*.

Wimco

Based in Rhode Island, Wimco oversees bookings for more than 230 properties, at $2,000–$10,000 a week for two- and three-bedroom villas and from $7,000 for larger villas. The website, which occasionally lists last-minute specials, has interactive floor plans, and a catalog is available by mail. The company can arrange for babysitters, massages, chefs, and other in-villa services as well as private air charters. ☎ *800/932–3222* ⊕ *www.wimco.com*.

Nightlife

Most of the nightlife in St. Barth is centered in Gustavia, though there are a few places to go outside of town. "In" clubs change from season to season, so you might ask around for the hot spot of the moment, but none really get going until about midnight. Theme parties are the current trend. Check the daily *St. Barth News* or *Le Journal de Saint-Barth* for details. A late (10 pm or later) reservation at one of the club–restaurants will eventually become a front-row seat at a party.

Shopping

St. Barth is a duty-free port, and its sophisticated visitors find shopping in its 200-plus boutiques a delight, especially for beach-wear, accessories, jewelry, and casual wear. It's no overstatement to say that shopping for fashionable clothing, jewels, and designer accessories is better in St. Barth than anywhere else in the Carib-bean. New shops open all the time, so there's always something to discover. Some stores close from noon to 3, but they are open until 7 pm. Many are closed on Sunday. A popular afternoon pastime is strolling the two major shopping areas in Gustavia and St-Jean. While high fashion is as pricey here as everywhere, French brands sell for up to 30% less than in the U.S.

For locally made art and handicrafts, the tourist office can provide information and arrange visits to studios of island artists, including Christian Bretoneiche, Robert Danet, Nathalie Daniel, Patricia Guyot, Rose Lemen, Aline de Lurin, and Marion Vinot. Gustavia, La Villa Créole, and the larger hotels have a few good gallery/craft boutiques.

Health and Safety

There's relatively little crime on St. Barth. Visitors can travel anywhere on the island with confidence. Most hotel rooms have safes for your valuables. As anywhere, don't tempt loss by leaving cameras, laptops, or jewelry out in plain sight in your hotel room or villa or in your car or car trunk. Also, don't walk barefoot at night: there are venomous centipedes that can inflict a remarkably painful sting. If you ask residents, they will tell you that they drink only bottled water, although most cook or make coffee with tap water.

Dengue, chikungunya, and zika have all been reported throughout the Caribbean. We recommend that you protect yourself from these mosquito-borne illnesses by keeping your skin covered and/or wearing mosquito repellent. The mosquitoes that transmit these viruses are as active by day as they are by night. Small hand-held mosquito zappers are available in some supermarkets.

Visitor Information

CONTACT Office du Tourisme. ☒ *Quai Général de Gaulle, Gustavia* ☎ *0590/27–87–27* ⊕ *www.saintbarth-tourisme.com*.

Gustavia

You can easily explore all of Gustavia during a two-hour stroll. Some shops close from noon to 3 or 4, so plan lunch accordingly, but stores stay open past 7 in the evening. Parking in Gustavia is a challenge, especially during vacation times. A good spot to park is rue de la République, alongside the catamarans, yachts, and sailboats.

◉ Sights

★ Le Musée Territorial, Wall House
MUSEUM | FAMILY | On the far side of the harbor known as La Pointe, the charming Municipal Museum on the first floor of the restored Wall House has watercolors, portraits, photographs, traditional costumes, and historic documents detailing the island's history over many hundreds of years, as well as displays of the island's flowers, plants, and marine life. There are also changing contemporary art exhibitions. It's a must-stop on your St. Barth visit, and it's free. ☒ *La Pointe, Gustavia* ☎ *0590/29–71–55* ⊕ *visitersaintbarthelemy.com/musee-territorial-de-gustavia* ☞ *Free*.

Le Petit Collectionneur
MUSEUM | Encouraged by family and friends, André Berry opened this private museum in his home to showcase his lifelong passion for collecting fascinating objects such as 18th-century English pipes and the first phonograph to come to the island. Today there are more than 1,000 pieces here, ranging from cannon balls to coins that are hundreds of years old. Berry will happily show you his treasures. ☒ *La Pointe, Gustavia* ☞ *€2*.

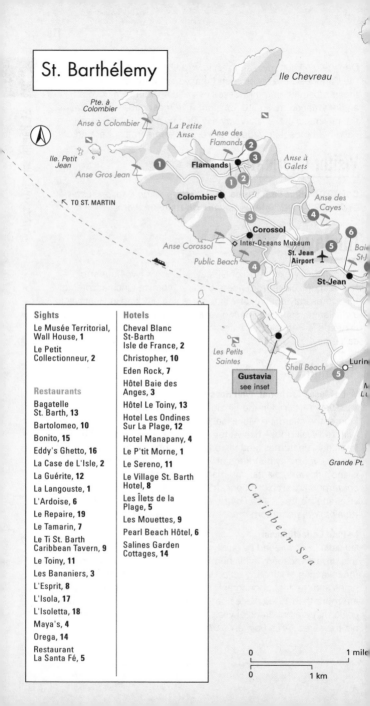

St. Barthélemy

Ile Chevreau

Pte. à Colombier
Anse à Colombier
La Petite Anse
Ile. Petit Jean
Anse Gros Jean
TO ST. MARTIN

Anse des Flamands **2** **3**
Flamands
Anse à Galets
1 **2**
Colombier
3
Anse des Cayes **4**
Corossol
Inter-Oceans Museum
Anse Corossol
St. Jean Airport
Public Beach **4**
6
5
Baie St-J
St-Jean

Les Petits Saintes
Gustavia see inset

Shell Beach
5
Lurin

M Lu

Grande Pt.

Caribbean Sea

Sights

Le Musée Territorial, Wall House, **1**

Le Petit Collectionneur, **2**

Restaurants

Bagatelle St. Barth, **13**

Bartolomeo, **10**

Bonito, **15**

Eddy's Ghetto, **16**

La Case de L'Isle, **2**

La Guérite, **12**

La Langouste, **1**

L'Ardoise, **6**

Le Repaire, **19**

Le Tamarin, **7**

Le Ti St. Barth Caribbean Tavern, **9**

Le Toiny, **11**

Les Bananiers, **3**

L'Esprit, **8**

L'Isola, **17**

L'Isoletta, **18**

Maya's, **4**

Orega, **14**

Restaurant La Santa Fé, **5**

Hotels

Cheval Blanc St-Barth Isle de France, **2**

Christopher, **10**

Eden Rock, **7**

Hôtel Baie des Anges, **3**

Hôtel Le Toiny, **13**

Hotel Les Ondines Sur La Plage, **12**

Hotel Manapany, **4**

Le P'tit Morne, **1**

Le Sereno, **11**

Le Village St. Barth Hotel, **8**

Les Îlets de la Plage, **5**

Les Mouettes, **9**

Pearl Beach Hôtel, **6**

Salines Garden Cottages, **14**

0		1 mile
0		1 km

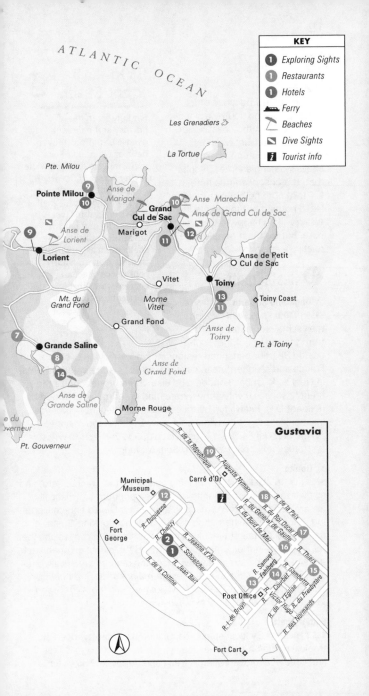

ATLANTIC OCEAN

Les Grenadiers

La Tortue

Pte. Milou

Pointe Milou 9
10

Anse de Marigot

Anse Marechal

**Grand
Cul de Sac** 10

Anse de Grand Cul de Sac

Marigot

12

9

Anse de Lorient

11

Lorient

Vitet

Anse de Petit Cul de Sac

Toiny 13

Mt. du Grand Fond

Morne Vitet

Toiny Coast

11

Grand Fond

Anse de Toiny

7

Pt. à Toiny

Grande Saline

8

Anse de Grand Fond

14

Anse de Grande Saline

Morne Rouge

e du
overneur

Pt. Gouverneur

KEY

- **1** Exploring Sights
- **1** Restaurants
- **1** Hotels
- Ferry
- Beaches
- Dive Sights
- *i* Tourist info

Gustavia

R. de la Republique

R. Auguste Nyman

19

Carré d'Or

i

18

R. de la Paix

R. du Roi Oscar II

Municipal Museum

12

R. Duquesna

R. du Bord de Mer

R. du Général de Gaulle

17

Fort George

2
1

R. Chanzy

R. Jeanne d'Arc

R. Schoelcher

R. Jean Bart

R. de la Colline

16

R. Thiers

R. Samuel Fahlberg

14

R. Gambetta

15

13

Post Office

R. Victor Hugo

R. Courbet

R. de l'Église

R. du Presbytère

R. I. de Bruyn

R. des Normands

Fort Cart

🏖 Beaches

Shell Beach

BEACH—SIGHT | Because of its rather sheltered southward-facing location on the coast south of downtown Gustavia, Shell Beach sees high numbers of shells washing ashore. Despite that, the unspoken rule here is "Take nothing but pictures, leave nothing but footprints." A taxi will be happy to take you here, but for most people it's a relatively easy walk.

🍴 Restaurants

★ Bagatelle St Barth

$$$$ | MODERN FRENCH | Watch the yachts on Gustavia harbor from the terrace of this sophisticated St-Tropez–inspired restaurant while enjoying cocktails and French and Mediterranean cuisine. Fans of sister establishments in New York, Dubai, London, and elsewhere will recognize the friendly service, lively atmosphere, and great music provided by resident DJs. **Known for:** haute cuisine in an elegant harborside location; late-night partying; chic crowd. ⓢ *Average main: €34* ✉ *Rue Samuel Fahlberg, Gustavia* ☏ *0590/27–51–51* ⊕ *www. bistrotbagatelle.com* ⊗ *Closed Sun. No lunch.*

★ Bonito

$$$$ | LATIN AMERICAN | Combining cuisines from France, Peru, and all over the Americas, Bonito delivers a spectrum of artistically assembled flavors, textures, and aromas that you'd find challenging to locate elsewhere. Located on a hill overlooking Gustavia harbor, the restaurant indulges you with big white canvas couches for lounging, in the center; tables around the sides; an open kitchen; and three bar areas. **Known for:** caring owners; artistically presented dishes; elegance. ⓢ *Average main: €45* ✉ *Rue Lubin Brin, Gustavia* ☏ *0590/27–96–96* ⊕ *www.ilovebonito.com* ⊗ *Closed Wed. and late Aug.–early Nov. No lunch.*

Eddy's Ghetto

$$$ | FRENCH | By local standards, dinner in the pretty, open-air, tropical garden here is reasonably priced. The cooking is French and Creole, and everything is fresh and delicious. **Known for:**

Picking the Right Beach 🏖

For long stretches of powder-soft pale sand choose La Saline, Gouverneur, or Flamands. For seclusion in nature, pick the tawny grains of Corossol. But the most remarkable beach on the island, Shell Beach, is right in Gustavia and hardly has sand at all! Millions of tiny pink shells wash ashore in drifts, thanks to an unusual confluence of ocean currents, sea-life beds, and hurricane action.

Gustavia Harbor welcomes ships to St. Barth.

beautiful tropical gardens; attentive service regardless of how busy they are; authentic French and local dishes. $ *Average main: €24* ⊠ *12 rue Samuel Fahlberg, Gustavia* ☎ *0590/27–54–17* ⊘ *Closed Sun. and Sept. and Oct. No lunch.*

La Guérite

$$$$ | **MEDITERRANEAN** | This stylish Greek-influenced restaurant, a sister of a well-beloved Cannes hot spot, is at the far side of Gustavia Harbor. The room is beautiful, overlooking the yachts; the service helpful and friendly; and the food is fresh, tasty, healthy, and well prepared, featuring many locally caught types of seafood. **Known for:** fish or veal carpaccios; wahoo, sea bass, mahimahi, tuna, and shrimp entrées; Black Angus rib eye. $ *Average main: €33* ⊠ *La Pointe, Gustavia* ☎ *0590/88–44–42* ⊕ *www.lague-rite-sbh.com.*

Le Repaire

$$ | **BRASSERIE** | **FAMILY** | Overlooking the harbor, this friendly classic French brasserie is busy from its 7 am opening to its late-night closing. The flexible hours are great if you arrive on the island midafternoon and need a substantial snack. **Known for:** St. Barth's only early breakfast restaurant; reliable any time of day; well-prepared, simple food. $ *Average main: €19* ⊠ *Rue de la République, Gustavia* ☎ *0590/27–72–48* ⊘ *Closed Sun.*

★ L'Isola

$$$$ | **ITALIAN** | The chic sister of Santa Monica, California's Via Veneto packs in happy guests for classic Italian dishes, dozens of house-made pasta dishes, prime meats, and a huge, well-chosen wine list. Restaurateur Fabrizio Bianconi wants it to feel like a big Italian party, and with all the celebrating in this pretty and romantic room, he has certainly succeeded. **Known for:** house-made pasta; festive atmosphere; the daily catch. $ *Average main: €38 ⊠ 33 rue du Roi Oscar II, Gustavia ☎ 0590/51–00–05 ⊕ www. lisolastbarth.com ��� Closed Sept. and Oct. No lunch.*

L'Isoletta

$$$ | **PIZZA** | This casual Roman-style pizzeria run by the popular L'Isola restaurant is a lively, chic lounge-style gastropub serving delicious thin-crust pizzas by the slice or the meter. There are even dessert pizzas, and excellent tiramisu. **Known for:** meter-long pizzas; lively atmosphere; wait times at peak hours. $ *Average main: €30 ⊠ Rue du Roi Oscar II, Gustavia ☎ 0590/52–02–02.*

Maya's

$$$$ | **CARIBBEAN** | New Englander Randy Gurley and his wife, Maya (a French-born chef), provide returning guests with a warm welcome and a very pleasant, albeit expensive, dinner on their cheerful deck overlooking Gustavia Harbor. A market-inspired menu of good, simply prepared and garnished dishes changes according to availability, one reason for the restaurant's ongoing popularity. **Known for:** friendly, attentive staff; great quality food; well worth the effort to find it. $ *Average main: €39 ⊠ Public, Gustavia ☎ 0590/27–75–73 ⊕ www.mayas-stbarth.com ��� Closed Sun. No lunch.*

★ Orega

$$$$ | **JAPANESE FUSION** | One of St. Barth's very best, this Franco-Japanese fusion restaurant draws legions of admirers for its top-notch sushi and fish, imported directly from sushi markets in Tokyo, New York, and Paris. The pretty room in which it's served is decorated in natural woods, neutral linen, and attractive art. **Known for:** extraordinary sushi and fish; outstanding service; Franco-Japanese fusions like green tea crème brûlée. $ *Average main: €41 ⊠ 13 rue Samuel Fahlberg, Gustavia ☎ 0590/52–45–31 ⊕ www.oregarestaurant.com ��� Closed Tues.*

🍸 Nightlife

Bar de l'Oubli

BARS/PUBS | This landmark, where locals and visitors mingle over drinks, is a good breakfast option, too (cash only). The service can be slow, though, so it's best if you're not in a hurry. ⊠ *Rue du Roi Oscar II, Gustavia ☎ 0590/27–70–06 ⊕ www.bardeloubli.com.*

Le Repaire
BARS/PUBS | This restaurant lures a crowd for cocktail hour and its pool table. It's great for dinner with a side of people-watching. ⊠ *Rue de la République, Gustavia* ☎ *0590/27–72–48.*

★ Le Sélect
BARS/PUBS | Quite possibly the inspiration for Jimmy Buffett's "Cheeseburger in Paradise," St. Barth's original hangout has been around since 1949. In the boisterous garden, the barefoot boating set gathers for a cold Carib beer at lower-than-usual prices while listening to a local band or DJ. And yes, you can grab a legendary "Cheeseburger in Paradise" here and not get indigestion when you see the surprisingly modest bill. ⊠ *Rue du Centenaire, Gustavia* ☎ *0590/27–86–87.*

🛍 Shopping

In Gustavia, boutiques pack the three major shopping streets. Quai de la République, which is right on the harbor, rivals New York's Madison Avenue or Paris's avenue Montaigne for high-end designer retail, including shops for **Louis Vuitton, Bulgari, Cartier, Chopard, Erès,** and **Hermès.** These shops often carry items that are not available in the United States. The elegant Carré d'Or plaza and the adjacent **Coeur Vendome** are great fun to explore. Shops are also clustered in **La Savane Commercial Center** (across from the airport), **La Villa Créole** (in St-Jean), and **Espace Neptune** (on the road to Lorient). It's worth working your way from one end to the other at these shopping complexes—just to see or, perhaps, be seen. Boutiques in all three areas carry the latest in French and Italian sportswear, charming children's togs, and some haute couture. Bargains may be tough to come by, but you might be able to snag that *Birkin* that has a long waiting list stateside, and in any case, you'll have a lot of fun hunting around.

BOOKS
La Case Aux Livres
BOOKS/STATIONERY | This full-service bookstore and newsstand has hundreds of English titles for adults and kids. Its blog lists author appearances, which may well be worth a stop if you're around. ⊠ *9 rue de la République, Gustavia* ☎ *0590/27–15–88* ⊕ *www.lacaseauxlivres.com.*

CLOTHING
Boutique Lacoste
CLOTHING | This store has a huge selection of the once-again-chic alligator-logo wear for men, women, and kids. ⊠ *Rue du Bord de Mer, Gustavia* ☎ *0590/27–66–90.*

Shoppers flock to Gustavia's Rue de France for high-end boutiques.

Hermès

CLOTHING | This independently owned franchise (closed September and October) has prices slightly below those in the States, a welcome notion among the sky-high prices here. ✉ *Rue de la République, Gustavia* ☎ *0590/27–66–15.*

Kokon

CLOTHING | This boutique offers a nicely edited mix of designs for on-island or off, including the bo'em, Lotty B. Mustique, and Day Birger lines, and cute shoes to go with them by Heidi Klum for Birkenstock. ✉ *Rue Samuel Fahlberg, Gustavia* ☎ *0590/29–74–48.*

Linen

CLOTHING | This shop offers tailored linen shirts for men in a rainbow of soft colors and soft slip-on driving mocs in classic styles. ✉ *Rue Lafayette, Gustavia* ☎ *0590/27–54–26* ⊕ *www.linensbh. com.*

Lolita Jaca

CLOTHING | This store has trendy, tailored sportswear and floaty silk charmeuse and cotton gauze tunics perfect for the beach. ✉ *Le Carré d'Or, Gustavia* ☎ *0590/27–59–98* ⊕ *www.lolitajaca.com.*

Mademoiselle Hortense

CLOTHING | Charming tops and dresses for the young and young at heart in pretty Liberty prints are made on the island. Great crafty bracelets and necklaces to accent your new styles are also here. ✉ *Rue de la République, Gustavia* ☎ *0590/27–13–29.*

Marina St. Barth

CLOTHING | The trendy, sexy resort wear here, worn by the young and the beautiful, ranges from floaty beachwear to Havaianas. Lines include Ondade and Façonnable, and there are unusual ponchos by Lotus London, high-fashion T-shirts by Eleven Paris, and elegant silk tunics by Jodé. ⊠ *Rue du Roi Oscar II, Gustavia* ☎ *0590/29–37–30* ⊕ *www.marina-stbarth.com.*

Pati de St Barth

CLOTHING | This is the largest of the three shops that stock the chic, locally made T-shirts, totes, and beach wraps that have become the de facto logo of St. Barth. The newest styles have hand-done graffiti-style lettering. The shop also has some handicrafts and other giftable items and great sandals. ⊠ *Rue du Bord de Mer, Gustavia* ☎ *0590/29–78–04* ⊕ *www.patidestbarth.com.*

Poupette St. Barth

CLOTHING | All the brilliant color-crinkle silk, chiffon batik, and embroidered peasant skirts and tops are designed by the owner. There also are great belts and beaded bracelets. ⊠ *Rue de la République, Gustavia* ☎ *0590/27–55–78* ⊕ *www.poupettestbarth. com.*

Saint-Barth Stock Exchange

CLOTHING | On the far side of Gustavia Harbor, the island's consignment and discount shop is a blast to explore. ⊠ *La Pointe, Gustavia* ☎ *0590/27–68–12.*

Vanita Rosa

CLOTHING | This store showcases beautiful lace and linen sundresses, peasant tops, plus bikinis, poncho/kaftans, accessories galore, and very cool designer vintage. ⊠ *Rue du Roi Oscar II, Gustavia* ☎ *0590/52–43–25* ⊕ *www.vanitarosa.com.*

Victoire

CLOTHING | Classic, well-made sportswear in luxurious fabrics and great colors has a French twist on preppy that plays as well in Nantucket and Greenwich as it does on St. Barth. A small sidewalk café has Wi-Fi and terrific *macarons*. ⊠ *Rue du Général de Gaulle, Gustavia* ☎ *0590/29–84–60* ⊕ *www.victoire.shop/en/ boutique/saint-barth-gustavia.*

FOODSTUFFS

A.M.C

FOOD/CANDY | This supermarket is a bit older than Marché U in St-Jean but can supply nearly anything you might need. It's closed Sunday. ⊠ *Quai de la République, Gustavia.*

HOME FURNISHINGS

French Indies Design

HOUSEHOLD ITEMS/FURNITURE | This beautiful shop on the far side of Gustavia Harbor is the brainchild of Karine Bruneel, a St. Barth–based architect and interior designer. There are lovely items to accent your home (or yacht) including furniture, textiles, glassware, and unusual decorative baskets, candles, and pottery. ⊠ *Maison Suédoise, Gustavia* ☎ *0590/29–66–38* ⊕ *www. frenchindiesdesign.fr.*

JEWELRY

Fabienne Miot

JEWELRY/ACCESSORIES | Unusual and artistic jewelry features rare stones and cultured pearls, watches, and jewelry. ⊠ *Rue de la République, Gustavia* ☎ *0590/27–73–13* ⊕ *www.fabiennemiot.com.*

Kalinas Perles

JEWELRY/ACCESSORIES | Beautiful freshwater pearls are knotted onto the classic St. Barth–style leather thongs by artist Jeremy Albaledejo, who also showcases other artisans' works. Tahitian black pearls are featured. ⊠ *23 rue du Général de Gaulle, Gustavia* ☎ *0690/65–93–00* ⊕ *www.kalinasperles.com.*

LEATHER GOODS AND ACCESSORIES

Human Steps

SHOES/LUGGAGE/LEATHER GOODS | This popular boutique stocks a well-edited selection of chic shoes and leather accessories from names like YSL, Prada, Balenciaga, Miu Miu, and Jimmy Choo. ⊠ *39 rue de la République, Gustavia* ☎ *0590/27–93–79* ⊕ *www. human-steps.fr.*

LIQUOR AND TOBACCO

La Cave du Port Franc

TOBACCO | This store has a huge selection of wine, especially from France. ⊠ *Rue de la République, Gustavia* ☎ *0590/27–65–27* ⊕ *www.lacaveduportfranc.com.*

Couleurs des Iles 120% Lino

TOBACCO | This shop has many rare varieties of smokables, including Cuban cigars, plus the original Panama hats, and good souvenir T-shirts, too. Head to the back for the stash of rare Puro Vintage. ⊠ *Rue du Général de Gaulle, Gustavia* ☎ *0590/27–79–20.*

M'Bolo

WINE/SPIRITS | Sample infused rums, including lemongrass, ginger, and the island favorite, vanilla, and bring some home in beautiful handblown bottles. Laguiole knives and local spices are sold, too, plus artisan products like homemade jam. ⊠ *Rue du Général de Gaulle, Gustavia* ☎ *0590/27–90–54* ⊕ *mbolo-rum.com/en.*

Anse de Toiny

Over the hills beyond Grand Cul de Sac is this much-photographed coastline. Stone fences crisscross the steep slopes of Morne Vitet, one of many small mountains on St. Barth, along a rocky shore that resembles the rugged coast of Normandy. Nicknamed the "washing machine" because of its turbulent surf, it is not recommended even to expert swimmers because of the strong undertow. ■TIP→ **There is a tough but scenic hike around the point. Take the road past Le Toiny hotel to the top to the start of the trail.**

🍽 Restaurants

Le Toiny
$$$$ | MODERN FRENCH | Hôtel Le Toiny's dramatic, redesigned, cliffside dining porch showcases nature and gastronomy in equal parts. The food is notable for its innovation and extraordinary presentation, and the warm but consummately professional service sets a high standard. **Known for:** exquisite views; attention to detail; relaxing setting. ⑤ *Average main: €47* ⊠ *Hôtel Le Toiny, Anse de Toiny* ☎ *0590/29–88–88* ⊕ *www.letoiny.com* ⊘ *Closed Sept.–mid-Oct.*

🛏 Hotels

★ Hôtel Le Toiny
$$$$ | HOTEL | Privacy, serenity, and personalized service please international sophisticates, who gravitate to this remote hotel since you never have to leave if you don't want to. **Pros:** extremely private; flawless service; environmental awareness. **Cons:** isolated (at least half an hour's drive from town); must take a hotel shuttle to reach the beach (though they're readily available). ⑤ *Rooms from: €1,545* ⊠ *Anse de Toiny* ☎ *0590/27–88–88* ⊕ *www.letoiny. com* ⊘ *Closed Sept.–late Oct.* ➶ *14 1-bedroom villas, 1 3-bedroom villa* ⍾ *Breakfast.*

Colombier

Beaches

Anse à Colombier
BEACH—SIGHT | The beach here is the island's least accessible, thus the most private; to reach it you must take either a rocky footpath from Petite Anse or brave the 30-minute climb down (and back

up) a steep, cactus-bordered trail from the top of the mountain behind the beach. Appropriate footgear is a must, and on the beach, the only shade is a rock cave. But this is a good place to snorkel. Boaters favor this cove for its calm anchorage. **Amenities:** none. **Best for:** snorkeling; swimming. ⊠ *Colombier*.

Restaurants

Les Bananiers

\$\$\$ | FRENCH | FAMILY | Ask the locals where to eat, and they will surely recommend this casual spot in Colombier, adjacent to a wonderful bakery. The food is classic French (though they're also well known for pizza), the service is warm, the prices are gentle (a rarity here), and you can eat in or take out. **Known for:** thin-crust pizza; reasonable prices; a can't-miss bakery next door. ⑤ *Average main: €23* ⊠ *Rte. de Colombier, Colombier* ☎ *0590/27–93–48.*

Hotels

Le P'tit Morne

\$ | B&B/INN | Each of the modestly furnished but clean and freshly decorated, painted mountainside studios has a private balcony with panoramic views of the coastline. **Pros:** reasonable rates; great area for hiking; helpful management. **Cons:** rooms are basic; remote location; not on the beach. ⑤ *Rooms from: €204* ⊠ *Colombier* ☎ *0590/52–95–50* ⥲ *14 rooms* ⭕ *Breakfast.*

Corossol

Traces of the island's French provincial origins are evident in this two-street fishing village with a little rocky beach. Stop for the scenery on the way up to Anse a Colombier; it's a 10-minute drive from Gustavia.

Flamands

Beaches

Anse des Flamands

BEACH—SIGHT | This is the most beautiful of the hotel beaches—a roomy strip of silken sand. Come here for lunch and then spend the afternoon sunning, enjoying long beach walks, and swimming in the turquoise water. From the beach, you can take a brisk hike along a paved sidewalk to the top of the now-extinct volcano believed to

Dinner at Le Toiny is private and romantic.

have given birth to St. Barth. **Amenities:** food and drink; toilets. **Best for:** snorkeling; swimming; walking. ⊠ *Anse des Flamands*.

🍴 Restaurants

★ La Case de L'Isle

$$$$ | **MODERN FRENCH** | You can't top the view or the service at this waterfront restaurant at the renowned Cheval Blanc St-Barth Isle de France, and at night there is no more romantic spot on the island. Lighter versions of traditional French fare are served. **Known for:** creative preparations; toes-in-the-sand dining; romantic ambience. ⑤ *Average main: €45* ⊠ *Cheval Blanc St-Barth Isle de France, Flamands Beach, Anse des Flamands* ☎ *0590/27–61–81* ⊕ *www.isle-de-france.com.*

La Langouste

$$$ | **FRENCH FUSION** | This small but friendly beachside restaurant in the pool courtyard of Hôtel Baie des Anges lives up to its name by serving fresh-grilled local lobster—and lobster thermidor—at prices that are somewhat gentler than at most other island venues. Try starters like local squash gratin, beef carpaccio, scallop-and-leek samosas, a warm goat cheese salad, or one of the five soups, including classic Caribbean fish soup and lobster bisque. **Known for:** pick-your-own lobster from the tank; lobster thermidor; classic French desserts. ⑤ *Average main: €26* ⊠ *Hôtel Baie des Anges, Anse des Flamands* ☎ *0590/27–63–61* ⊕ *www.hotel-baie-des-anges.com* ⊘ *Closed late Aug.–mid-Oct.*

🛏 Hotels

⭐ Cheval Blanc St-Barth Isle de France

$$$$ | **RESORT** | Nestled along a pristine white-sand beach, in tropical gardens, or on a hillside, the spacious rooms, suites, and villas of this intimate, casual, and refined resort are private and luxurious. **Pros:** prime beach location; excellent restaurant; great spa. **Cons:** car needed to get around; pricey, like everything on the island. ⑤ *Rooms from: €935* ✉ *B.P. 612 Baie des Flamands, Anse des Flamands* ☎ *0590/27–61–81* ⊕ *www.chevalblanc.com* ⊘ *Closed Sept.–mid-Oct.* ⊃ *40 units* ⦿ *Breakfast.*

Hôtel Baie des Anges

$$ | **HOTEL** | **FAMILY** | Everyone is treated like family at this casual retreat with 10 clean, spacious units, two of which are completely renovated, modern two-bedroom oceanfront suites, one with a Jacuzzi. **Pros:** on St. Barth's longest beach; family-friendly; excellent value. **Cons:** a bit remote from town, so you'll need a car; not super fancy; the boutique is good but not likely to cover all your shopping needs. ⑤ *Rooms from: €300* ✉ *Anse des Flamands* ☎ *0590/27–63–61* ⊕ *www.hotel-baie-des-anges.com* ⊘ *Closed Sept.* ⊃ *10 rooms* ⦿ *No meals.*

Gouverneur

⛱ Beaches

Anse du Gouverneur

BEACH—SIGHT | **FAMILY** | Because it's so secluded, this beach continues to be a popular place for nude sunbathing. Truly beautiful, it has blissful swimming and views of St. Kitts, Saba, and St. Eustatius. Venture here at the end of the day and watch the sun set behind the hills. The road here from Gustavia also offers spectacular vistas. Legend has it that pirates' treasure is buried in the vicinity. There are no restaurants, toilets, or other services here, so plan accordingly. **Amenities:** parking (no fee). **Best for:** nudists; sunset; swimming; walking. ✉ *Le Gouverneur.*

Grand Cul de Sac

Beaches

Anse de Grand Cul de Sac

BEACH—SIGHT | FAMILY | The shallow, reef-protected beach is nice for small children, fly-fishermen, kayakers, and windsurfers—and for the amusing frigate birds that dive-bomb the water fishing for their lunch. You needn't do your own fishing; you can have a wonderful lunch at one of the excellent restaurants nearby and use their lounge chairs for the afternoon. You may see some turtles in the shallow water. After storms the water may be a bit murky. **Amenities:** food and drink; parking (no fee); toilets; water sports. **Best for:** swimming; walking. ⊠ *Grand Cul de Sac.*

 Restaurants

Bartolomeo

$$$$ | ECLECTIC | FAMILY | Locavores will like the refined cuisine at this pretty restaurant in the gardens of the Guanahani hotel. Influenced by Provence and Italy, beautifully presented dishes use some organic and local products. **Known for:** local ingredients; beautiful setting; catch-your-own dinner excursion. ⑤ *Average main: €43* ⊠ *Hotel Guanahani, Grand Cul de Sac* ☎ *0590/27–66–60* ⊙ *Closed Thurs. No lunch.*

🛏 Hotels

Hotel Les Ondines Sur La Plage

$$$ | RENTAL | FAMILY | Right on the beach, this reasonably priced, intimate gem comprises modern, comfortable apartments with room to spread out. **Pros:** close to restaurants and water sports; nice pool; airport transfers included. **Cons:** not a resort; narrow beach; you'll need a car. ⑤ *Rooms from: €450* ⊠ *Grand Cul de Sac* ☎ *0590/27–69–64* ⊕ *www.st-barths.com/les-ondines* ⊙ *Closed Sept.–mid-Oct.* 🛏 *7 units* ⦿ *Breakfast.*

★ Le Sereno

$$$$ | RESORT | Those seeking a restorative, sensuous escape discover nirvana at the quietly elegant, aptly named Le Sereno, set on a beachy cove of turquoise sea, between the island's highest mountain and the foamy waves. **Pros:** beach location; super-chic comfort; renovated from top to bottom after Hurricane Irma. **Cons:** air-conditioning may not extend to bathrooms; likely to spoil you for other places; enables total relaxation. ⑤ *Rooms from: €870* ⊠ *B.P. 19 Grand-Cul-de-Sac, Grand Cul de Sac*

☎ *0590/29–83–00* ⊕ *www. lesereno.com* ⊗ *Closed late Aug.–mid-Oct.* ⇌ *37 units* ⓘ⊙ *Some meals.*

Grande Saline

🏖 Beaches

★ Anse de Grande Saline

BEACH—SIGHT | With its peaceful seclusion and sandy ocean bottom, this is just about everyone's favorite beach and is great for swimming, too. Without any major development, it's an ideal Caribbean strand, though there can be a bit of wind at times. In spite of the prohibition, young and old alike go nude. The beach is a 10-minute walk up a rocky dune trail, so wear sneakers or water shoes, and bring a blanket, umbrella, and beach towels. There are several good lunch restaurants near the parking area, but the beach itself is just sand, sea, and sky. The big salt ponds here are no longer in use, and the place looks a little desolate on approach, but don't despair. **Amenities:** parking (no fee). **Best for:** nudists; swimming; walking. ⊠ *Grande Saline.*

🍴 Restaurants

★ L' Esprit

$$$$ | **MODERN FRENCH** | **FAMILY** | Renowned chef Jean-Claude Dufour (formerly of Eden Rock) brings innovative dishes to a romantic terrace close to Saline Beach. The menu has lots of variety, from light French dishes with a Provençal twist to interesting salads that have included soba noodles with shrimp and lime to dishes such as roasted pigeon with foie gras, steak, and vegetarian options. **Known for:** creative menu items; outstanding service; excellent wine list. ⑤ *Average main: €38* ⊠ *Anse de Grande Saline, Grande Saline* ☎ *0590/52–46–10* ⊗ *Closed Sun. and Mon. No lunch.*

★ Le Tamarin

$$$$ | **INTERNATIONAL** | With a beautiful tropical garden that shades the lounge chairs surrounding the palapa of the restaurant, Tamarin is tops for dinner near Grande Saline Beach. The service is attentive and friendly, and the wine list is excellent. **Known for:** superb outdoor dining; variety of entrées; great service.

🛏 Hurricane Recovery

Like many Caribbean islands, St. Barth was hit badly by Hurricane Irma in 2017. Since that time, many of the luxury villas and hotels took the opportunity to completely renovate.

§ *Average main: €42* ⊠ *Grande Saline, Grande Saline* ☎ *0590/29–27–74* ⊕ *www.tamarinstbarth.com* ☉ *Closed Mon.*

Restaurant La Santa Fé

$$$$ | **FRENCH** | **FAMILY** | Perched at the top of the Lurin hills on the way to Gouverneur Beach, this relaxed and scenic restaurant serves panoramic views with both lunch and dinner. The chef comes from Provence and trained at some of its best restaurants before moving to the Caribbean. **Known for:** incredible views of neighboring islands; beautiful presentation; generous portions. § *Average main: €34* ⊠ *Rte. de Lurin, Lurin* ☎ *0590/27–61–04* ☉ *Closed Tues., Wed., and Sept.–mid-Oct.*

🛏 Hotels

Salines Garden Cottages

$ | **RENTAL** | **FAMILY** | Budget-conscious beach lovers who don't require a lot of coddling need look no further than these petite garden cottages, a short stroll from St. Barth's best beach. **Pros:** only property walkable to Grande Saline Beach; quiet; good restaurants nearby. **Cons:** far from town; not very private; strict cancellation policy. § *Rooms from: €220* ⊠ *Grande Saline* ☎ *0590/51–04–44* ⊕ *www.salinesgarden.com* ☉ *Closed mid-Aug.–mid-Oct.* ⌁ *5 cottages* ⦿ *Breakfast.*

Lorient

🏝 Beaches

Anse de Lorient

BEACH—SIGHT | **FAMILY** | This beach is popular with families and surfers, who like its waves and central location. Be aware of the level of the tide, which can come in very quickly. Hikers and avid surfers like the walk over the hill to Pointe Milou in the late afternoon, when the waves roll in. **Amenities:** parking (no fee). **Best for:** snorkeling; surfing; swimming. ⊠ *Lorient.*

🛏 Hotels

Les Mouettes

$ | **RENTAL** | **FAMILY** | This guesthouse offers clean, simply furnished, and economical bungalows with kitchenettes that open directly onto the beach but are also very close to the road. **Pros:** on the beach; family-friendly; less expensive than many St. Barth options. **Cons:** basic rooms without TVs; strict prepayment and cancellation policies; no pool, but you're on the beach. $ *Rooms from: €207* ✉ *Lorient* ☎ *0590/27–77–91* ⊕ *www.lesmouetteshotel.com* ▤ *No credit cards* ⇆ *7 bungalows* ⍾ *No meals.*

💼 Shopping

COSMETICS

Ligne St. Barth

PERFUME/COSMETICS | Superb skin-care products are made on-site from local tropical plants. Call to request a visit from a beautician or therapist to your villa or yacht. ✉ *Rte. de Saline, Lorient* ☎ *0590/27–82–63* ⊕ *www.lignestbarth.com.*

FOODSTUFFS

JoJo Supermarché

FOOD/CANDY | This well-stocked counterpart to Gustavia's supermarket gets daily deliveries of bread and produce. JoJoBurger, next door, is the local surfers' spot for a (very good) quick burger. ✉ *Lorient* ☎ *0590/27–63–53.*

Pointe Milou

🍽 Restaurants

⭐ Le Ti St. Barth Caribbean Tavern

$$$$ | **ECLECTIC** | Chef-owner Carole Gruson captures the island's funky, sexy spirit in her wildly popular hilltop spot. Come to dance to great music with the attractive bar crowd, lounge at a pillow-strewn banquette, or chat on the torch-lighted terrace. **Known for:** fun nights from beginning to end; lively crowd; legendary barbecue. $ *Average main: €53* ✉ *Pointe Milou* ☎ *0590/27–97–71* ⊕ *www.tistbarth.com.*

🛏 Hotels

⭐ Christopher

$$$$ | **RESORT** | **FAMILY** | This longtime favorite of European families delivers a high standard of professionalism and courteous service. **Pros:** comfortable elegance; family-friendly; reasonable pricing. **Cons:** on the water but not on a beach; three-night minimum; there's a bit of walking to get around the complex. $ *Rooms from: €595* ✉ *Pointe Milou* ☎ *0590/27–63–63* ⊕ *www.hotelchristopher. com* ☾ *Closed Sept.–mid-Oct.* ⇆ *42 rooms* ⍾ *Breakfast.*

St. Barth's Spas 🛌

Visitors to St. Barth can enjoy more than the comforts of home by taking advantage of the myriad wellness, spa, and beauty treatments available on the island. Major hotels—the Cheval Blanc St-Barth Isle de France and Christopher among them—have beautiful, comprehensive, on-site spas. Others, including Le Village St. Barth Hotel, Le Sereno, and Hôtel Le Toiny, have added spa cottages, where treatments and services can be arranged on-site. Depending on availability, all island visitors can book services at these locations. There's a new wellness retreat here, with metabolic and detox programs available. In addition, scores of independent therapists will come to your hotel room or villa and provide any therapeutic discipline you can think of, including yoga, Thai massage, shiatsu, reflexology, and even manicures, pedicures, and hairdressing. You can get recommendations at the tourist office in Gustavia.

St-Jean

There is a monument at the crest of the hill that divides St-Jean from Gustavia. Called *The Arawak,* it symbolizes the soul of St. Barth. A warrior, one of the earliest inhabitants of the area (AD 800–1,800) holds a lance in his right hand and stands on a rock shaped like the island; in his left hand he holds a conch shell, which sounds the cry of nature; perched beside him are a pelican (which symbolizes the air and survival by fishing) and an iguana (which represents the earth). The half-mile-long crescent of sand at St-Jean is the island's favorite beach. A popular activity is watching and photographing the hair-raising airplane landings (but it is *extremely* dangerous to stand at the beach end of the runway). Some of the best shopping on the island is here as are several restaurants.

 Beaches

Baie de St-Jean
BEACH—SIGHT | FAMILY | Like a mini Côte d'Azur—beachside bistros, terrific shopping, bungalow hotels, bronzed bodies, windsurfing, and day-trippers who tend to arrive on *big* yachts—the reef-protected strip is divided by the Eden Rock promontory. Except when the hotels are filled, you can rent chaises and umbrellas at the Pearl Beach restaurant or Eden Rock (reopened 2019), where you

The secluded beach at Eden Rock is a sunbather's dream.

can lounge for hours over lunch. **Amenities:** food and drink; toilets. **Best for:** partiers; walking. ⊠ *St-Jean.*

 Restaurants

L'Ardoise

\$\$ | **FRENCH** | Sit at a shaded communal table at this lively, modern gastropub/wine bar in St-Jean's Villa Creole shopping enclave any time of the day. Come for first-rate sharing platters of charcuterie, pâté, artisanal cheeses, and sweet or savory crepes. **Known for:** perfect place to make new friends; reasonable prices; generous portions. ⑤ *Average main: €16* ⊠ *La Villa Créole, St-Jean* ☎ *0590/77–41–97* ⊕ *www.lardoise.restaurant.*

🛏 Hotels

★ Eden Rock

\$\$\$\$ | **RESORT** | **FAMILY** | This iconic luxury hotel on the top of a rocky promontory over St-Jean reopened late in 2019 after major post-Irma renovations. **Pros:** chic clientele; beach setting; stylish facilities. **Cons:** some suites near street are noisy; some construction or site work may continue for a bit; car needed to tour the entire island. ⑤ *Rooms from: €1,500* ⊠ *Baie de St-Jean, St-Jean* ☎ *0590/29–79–99, 877/563–7015 in U.S.* ⊕ *www.edenrockhotel. com* ⊗ *Closed Sept 1.–mid-Oct.* ⇨ *35 units* ¶◎¶ *Free Breakfast.*

★ **Hotel Manapany**

$$$$ | **RESORT** | On a private beach of Anse de Cayes, this breezy yet luxurious B Signature resort (the first outside of mainland France) is an eco-friendly paradise, with solar panels and electric cars on property. **Pros:** five minutes to the airport with complimentary transfers; spa faces the sea; open-air restaurant. **Cons:** not in the action of Baie St-Jean. $ *Rooms from: €550* ⊠ *Anse de Cayes, St-Jean* 🕿 *590 27 66 55* ⊕ *hotelmanapany-stbarth.com* ⤳ *43 villas and suites* ⦿ *No meals.*

★ **Le Village St. Barth Hotel**

$$ | **HOTEL** | **FAMILY** | For two generations the Charneau family has offered friendly hotel service, villa advantages, and reasonable rates, making guests feel like a part of the family. **Pros:** convenient location; wonderful management; on-site spa and gym. **Cons:** steep walk to hotel, many steps; rooms close to street can be noisy. $ *Rooms from: €350* ⊠ *Colline de St-Jean, St-Jean* 🕿 *0590/27–61–39, 800/651–8366* ⊕ *www.levillagestbarth.com* ⤳ *28 units* ⦿ *Free Breakfast.*

Les Îlets de la Plage

$$$ | **RENTAL** | **FAMILY** | On the far side of the airport and the far corner of Baie de St-Jean, these well-priced, island-style one-, two-, and three-bedroom bungalows are nestled either on the beach itself or among lush tropical gardens on the hillside, with stunning views of the Bay. The units have small kitchens, open-air sitting areas, and comfortable bathrooms. **Pros:** beach location; apartment conveniences; front porches. **Cons:** TVs by request and with limited French programming; limited air conditioning; next to airport, so you will hear some small planes taking off. $ *Rooms from: €465* ⊠ *Plage de St-Jean, St-Jean* 🕿 *0590/27–88–57* ⊕ *www.lesilets.com* ☾ *Closed Sept. and Oct.* ⤳ *12 units* ⦿ *Breakfast.*

Pearl Beach Hôtel

$$ | **HOTEL** | Formerly Le Tom Beach Hotel, this chic but casual boutique property on busy St-Jean beach is fun for social types; the nonstop house party may well spill onto the terraces and last into the wee hours. **Pros:** party central at beach, restaurant, and pool; in town; many places of interest are walking distance away. **Cons:** trendy social scene is not for everybody, especially light sleepers; some noise from the airport; you'll need a car to get to other beaches. $ *Rooms from: €320* ⊠ *Plage de St-Jean, St-Jean* 🕿 *0590/52–81–20* ⊕ *pearlbeachstbarth.com* ⤳ *12 rooms* ⦿ *Free Breakfast.*

🍸 Nightlife

Le Nikki Beach

BARS/PUBS | This place rocks on weekends at lunch—especially Sunday—when the scantily clad young and beautiful lounge on the white canvas banquettes. ⊠ *St-Jean* ☎ *0590/27–64–64* ⊕ *www.nikkibeach.com.*

👜 Shopping

CLOTHING

Bamboo St. Barth

CLOTHING | Beach fashions like cotton tunics, cocktails-on-the-yacht dresses, and sexy Australian swimsuits by Nicole Olivier and Seafolly can be paired with sassy sandals and costume jewelry. ⊠ *Pelican Beach, St-Jean* ☎ *0690/52–08–82* ⊕ *www.facebook. com/bamboo.stbarth.*

Black Swan

CLOTHING | This shop has an unparalleled selection of bathing suits, and it also offers beach dresses, hats, caps, and sunglasses. ⊠ *La Villa Créole, St-Jean* ☎ *0590/52–48–30.*

Cabane Saint-Barth

CLOTHING | Stocked with stenciled cotton, gauzy beach tops, great straw fedoras, caftans (for all ages), plus beachy shoes and accessories, this shop is open nonstop every day. ⊠ *Pelican Beach, St-Jean* ☎ *0590/51–21–02.*

Filles des Iles

CLOTHING | In addition to high-quality, flattering French attire and sophisticated swimwear that even women of a certain age can wear, this shop stocks delicious artisanal fragrances and chic accessories, like beautiful sandals. ⊠ *8 Villa Créole, St-Jean* ☎ *0590/29–04–08.*

Iléna

CLOTHING | Incredible beachwear and lingerie by Chantal Thomas, Sarda, and others includes Swarovski crystal–encrusted bikinis for the young and gorgeous. ⊠ *La Villa Créole, St-Jean* ☎ *0590/29–84–05.*

KIWI St. Tropez

CLOTHING | This popular resortwear boutique for women, men, and kids has a branch in Gustavia, too. In addition to beachwear for everyone, they carry a variety of beach bags and towels. ⊠ *3 Villa Créole, St-Jean* ☎ *0590/27–57–08* ⊕ *www.kiwi.fr.*

Lili Belle
CLOTHING | Their great selection includes chic, French designer beachwear and resort clothing. ✉ *Pelican Beach, St-Jean* ☎ *0590/87–46–14.*

Morgan
CLOTHING | Great selection of trendy women's clothing, accessories, shoes, hats, bags, and more. ✉ *La Villa Créole, St-Jean* ☎ *0590/27–57–22.*

SUD SUD.ETC.
CLOTHING | This store stocks bags, beachy shell jewelry, as well as gauzy cover-ups. ✉ *La Villa Creole, St-Jean.*

FOODSTUFFS
Marché U
CONVENIENCE/GENERAL STORES | This modern, fully stocked supermarket across from the airport has a wide selection of French cheeses, pâtés, cured meats, produce, fresh bread, wine, and liquor. There is also a good selection of prepared foods and organic items. It's closed Sunday afternoon. ✉ *Face à l'aéroport, St-Jean* ☎ *0590/27–68–16.*

Maya's to Go
FOOD/CANDY | This is the place to go for prepared picnics, meals, salads, and rotisserie chickens from the kitchen of the popular restaurant in Gustavia. The emphasis is on freshness, so menu items change according to season and availability. This is not your average "boxed lunch" place; you could well get wahoo ceviche here, fresh of course, depending on the daily catch. ✉ *Les Galeries du Commerce, St-Jean* ☎ *0590/29–83–70* ⊕ *www.mayastogo.com* ☾ *Closed Mon.*

Activities

Boating and Sailing

St. Barth is a popular yachting and sailing center, thanks to its location midway between Antigua and St. Thomas.

Gustavia's harbor, 13 to 16 feet deep, has mooring and docking facilities for 40 yachts. There are also good anchorages at Public, Corossol, and Colombier. You can charter sailing and motorboats in Gustavia Harbor for as little as a half day, staffed or bareboat. Ask at the Gustavia tourist office or your hotel for a list of recommended charter companies.

Carib Waterplay

BOATING | On St. Jean beach for over 35 years, this outfit lets you try windsurfing, kayaking, and stand-up paddling; rents waterbikes; and gives kids' windsurf lessons. You can rent beach chairs for the day here. ⊠ *St-Jean* ☏ *0690/61–80–81* ⊕ *www.caribwaterplay.com*.

Jicky Marine Service

BOATING | This company offers private full-day outings on motorboats, Zodiacs, and 42- or 46-foot catamarans to the uninhabited Île Fourchue for swimming, snorkeling, cocktails, or lunch, as well as scheduled cruises including weekly half- and full-day group cruises and twice-weekly group sunset catamaran cruises. Private fishing charters are also offered, as is private transport from St. Martin. Skippered motorboat rentals run about €1,400 per day. A one-hour group Jet Ski tour of the island is also offered, as are private tours. ⊠ *26 rue Jeanne D'Arc, Gustavia* ☏ *0590/27–70–34* ⊕ *www.jickymarine.com*.

St Barth Sailing

SAILING | Captain Eric offers his 47' sailing catamaran *Okeanos* for day trips for up to 16 people and charters for up to six. Half-day, full-day, and sunset-champagne cruises are available with all the amenities you could ask for either standard or available, or you can charter the boat and sail to the British Virgin Islands, Antigua and Barbuda, or St. Martin and Anguila, all available as seven-day, six-night sailing adventures. ☏ *690/19–00–15* ⊕ *saintbarthsailing.com*.

St Barth Sailor

SAILING | Want to rent a bareboat or crewed catamaran and take off for your own tour of several islands? Captain Miguel Danet enables you to do exactly that, for a full-day, half-day, or sunset cruise. Extras are available, from special dining choices aboard to massage to scuba to underwater scooters. ☏ *690/18–60–66* ⊕ *www.stbarthsailor.com*.

Top Loc Boat Rental

BOATING | Charter a catamaran for a day of fun on the water. Rental for a half-day on the catamaran including an open bar is €580. Other rates / itineraries available. ⊠ *Airport Office, St-Jean* ☏ *0590/29–02–02* ⊕ *www.top-loc.com*.

Diving and Snorkeling

Several dive shops arrange scuba excursions. Depending on weather conditions, you may dive at **Pain de Sucre, Coco Island,** or toward nearby **Saba.** There's also an underwater shipwreck, plus sharks, rays, sea tortoises, coral, and the usual varieties of colorful fish. The waters on the island's leeward side are the calmest. For the uncertified, there's a shallow reef right off the beach at Anse de Cayes, which you can explore with mask and fins, and a hike down to the beach at Corossol brings you to a very popular snorkeling spot.

Ouanalao Dive

DIVING/SNORKELING | This well-regarded company offers PADI and CMAS, night dives, private dives and snorkeling, rental of fins, mask and snorkel, and more. Organized dives, a good dive shop, and instruction are offered at the Grand Cul-de Sac beach location. A two-tank dive is €150. A two-hour snorkeling trip to a nearby island starts at €65 per person. ⊠ *Grand Cul de Sac* ☎ *0690/63–74–34* ⊕ *www.ouanalaodive.com.*

Plongée Caraïbea

DIVING/SNORKELING | **FAMILY** | This company is recommended for its up-to-the-minute equipment, dive boat, and scuba discovery program. They offer nitrox diving and certification, and they also run two-hour group snorkeling trips on the *Blue Cat Catamaran* (€60 per person), or you can enjoy a private charter from €690. ⊠ *Quai de la République, Gustavia* ☎ *0590/27–55–94* ⊕ *www. plongee-caraibes.com.*

Réserve Naturelle de Saint-Barthélemy

SCUBA DIVING | Most of the waters surrounding St. Barth are protected in the island's nature reserve, which provides informa-tion from its Gustavia office. The diving here isn't nearly as rich as in more dive-centered destinations like Saba and St. Eustatius (Statia), but the options aren't bad either. ⊠ *Gustavia* ☎ *0590/27–88–18* ⊕ *www.reservenaturellestbarth.com.*

Splash

SCUBA DIVING | This company offers PADI and CMAS (Confédéra-tion Mondiale des Activités Subaquatiques—World Underwater Federation) diver training at all levels. Instructors speak French and English. Although the boat normally leaves daily at 9, 11:30, 2, and in the evening for a night dive, times are adjusted to suit preferences. Seabob scuba scooters are available at reasonable rates. ⊠ *Gustavia* ☎ *0590/56–90–24.*

Fishing

Most fishing is done in the waters north of Lorient, Flamands, and Corossol. Popular catches are tuna, marlin, wahoo, and barracuda. The annual St. Barth Open Fishing Tournament, organized by Océan Must, is in mid-July.

Guided Tours

You can arrange island tours by minibus or car at hotel desks or through taxi operators in Gustavia or at the airport. The tourist office runs a variety of tours for about €50 for a half day for up to eight people. You can also download up-to-the-minute walking and driving tour itineraries from the office's website.

Helene Bernier

TOUR—SPORTS | Helene does complete island tours of St. Barth. She's a native and a member of the island council. ☎ *690/63–46–09.*

JC Taxi

TOUR—SPORTS | Since 1986, native-born Jean-Claude has been providing safe and comfortable transportation in a 10-passenger minivan. Island tours and night driving are available. ✉ *Gustavia* ☎ *0690/49–02–97.*

St. Barth Mobilité

SPECIAL-INTEREST | This company offers transportation, tours, and guided help for those with limited mobility. ☎ *0690/77–66–73* ⊕ *www.stbarthmobilite.com.*

Chapter 5

ANGUILLA

Updated by
Jeff Berger

⊙ Sights	🍴 Restaurants	🛏 Hotels	🛍 Shopping	🍸 Nightlife
★★★★☆	★★★★☆	★★★★☆	★★★☆☆	★★★☆☆

WELCOME TO ANGUILLA

TOP REASONS TO GO

★ **Beautiful Beaches:** Miles of brilliant beach ensure you have a high-quality spot on which to lounge.

★ **Great Restaurants:** The dining scene offers both fine dining and delicious casual food on and off the beach.

★ **Fun, Low-Key Nightlife:** A funky late-night local music scene features reggae and string bands.

★ **Upscale Accommodations:** Excellent luxury resorts coddle you in comfort.

★ **Hidden Bargains:** You'll find a few relative bargains for both food and lodging if you look hard enough.

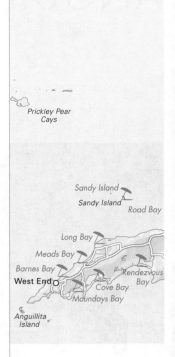

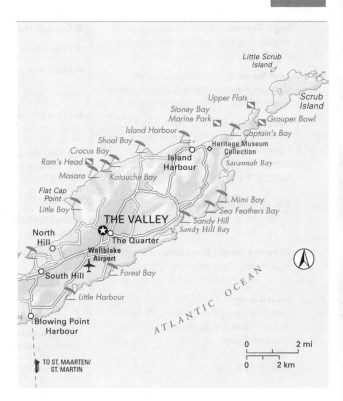

Little Scrub
Island

Scrub
Island

Upper Flats

Stoney Bay
Marine Park

Grouper Bowl

Island Harbour

Captain's Bay

Shoal Bay

Heritage Museum
Collection

Crocus Bay

Island
Harbour

Savannah Bay

Ram's Head

Masara

Katouche Bay

Flat Cap
Point

Mimi Bay

Little Bay

Sea Feathers Bay

THE VALLEY

Sandy Hill
Sandy Hill Bay

North
Hill

The Quarter

Wallblake
Airport

South Hill

Forest Bay

ATLANTIC OCEAN

Little Harbour

Blowing Point
Harbour

TO ST. MAARTEN/
ST. MARTIN

0   2 mi

0   2 km

ISLAND SNAPSHOT

WHEN TO GO

High Season: Mid-December through mid-April is the most fashionable and most expensive time to visit.

Low Season: From August to late October, temperatures can grow oppressively hot and the weather muggy.

Value Season: From late April to July and again November to mid-December, hotel prices drop 20% to 50%.

WAYS TO SAVE

Eat at roadside vendors. Head to "The Strip" in The Valley for local food trucks, or try one of the weekend pop-up BBQs.

Stay in a beach bungalow. Several local hotels have retained a true West Indian flair and lower prices.

Beach it up. All beaches on Anguilla are free and open to the public; the best include Meads Bay, Rendezvous Bay, and Shoal Bay.

BIG EVENTS

March: Musicians join together in the annual Moonsplash music festival. ⊕ www.olaidebanks.wix.com

March–April: Celebrate Anguilla culture during Easter weekend's Festival del Mar. ⊕ www.ivisitanguilla.com

May: The national love for boat racing peaks at the annual Anguilla Regatta. ⊕ www.anguillaregatta.com

July–August: Anguilla Summer Fest features two weeks of pageants, parades, and fireworks.

AT A GLANCE

■ **Capital:** The Valley

■ **Population:** 15,045

■ **Currency:** Eastern Caribbean dollar; pegged to U.S. dollar

■ **Money:** Some ATMs are closed weekends; credit cards accepted; U.S. dollar widely accepted

■ **Language:** English

■ **Country Code:** ☏ 1 264

■ **Emergencies:** ☏ 911

■ **Driving:** On the left

■ **Electricity:** 110v/60 cycles; plugs are U.S. standard two-prong

■ **Time:** Same as New York during daylight saving time; one hour ahead otherwise

■ **Documents:** A valid passport and must have a return or ongoing ticket

■ **Major Mobile Companies:** LIME, Digicel

■ **Anguilla Tourist Office:** ⊕ www.ivisitanguilla.com

Peace, pampering, great food, and a wonderful local music scene are among the star attractions on Anguilla (pronounced an-*gwill*-a). Beach lovers may become giddy when they first spot the island from the air; its blindingly white sand and lustrous blue-and-aquamarine waters are mesmerizing. And if you like sophisticated cuisine served in casually elegant open-air settings, this may well become your culinary Shangri-la.

The island's name, a reflection of its shape, is most likely a derivative of *anguille,* which is French for "eel." (French explorer Pierre Laudonnaire is credited with having given the island this name when he sailed past it in 1556.) In 1631 the Dutch built a fort here, but so far no one has been able to locate its site. English settlers from St. Kitts colonized the island in 1650, with plans to cultivate tobacco and, later, cotton and then sugar. But the thin soil and scarce water doomed these enterprises. Except for a brief period of independence, when it broke from its association with St. Kitts and Nevis in the late 1960s, Anguilla has remained a British colony ever since.

From the early 1800s various island federations were formed and disbanded, with Anguilla all the while simmering over its subordinate status and forced union with St. Kitts. Anguillians twice petitioned for direct rule from Britain and twice were ignored. In 1967, when St. Kitts, Nevis, and Anguilla became an associated state, the mouse roared; citizens kicked out St. Kitts's policemen, held a self-rule referendum, and for two years conducted their own affairs. To what *Time* magazine called "a cascade of laughter around the world," a British "peacekeeping force" of 100 paratroopers from the Elite Red Devil unit parachuted onto the island, squelching Anguilla's designs for autonomy but helping a team of royal engineers stationed there to improve the port and build roads and schools. Today Anguilla elects a House of Assembly and its own leader to handle internal affairs, and a British governor is responsible for public service, the police, the judiciary, and external affairs. Some tourists may still be wondering whose responsibility it is to repair roads, some of which are absolute patchworks.

The territory of Anguilla includes a few islets (or cays, pronounced "keys"), such as Scrub Island, Dog Island, Prickly Pear Cay, Sandy Island, and Sombrero Island. The 15,000 or so island residents are predominantly of African descent, but there are also many of Irish background, whose ancestors came from St. Kitts in the 1600s. Historically, because the limestone land was unfit for agriculture, attempts at enslavement never lasted long; consequently, Anguilla doesn't bear the scars of slavery found on so many other Caribbean islands. Instead, Anguillians became experts at making a living from the sea and are known for their boatbuilding and fishing skills. Tourism is the stable economy's growth industry, but the government carefully regulates expansion to protect the island's natural resources and beauty. New hotels are relatively small, select, casino-free, and generally expensive; Anguilla emphasizes its high-quality service, serene surroundings, and friendly people.

Planning

Getting Here and Around

AIR TRAVEL

There are no nonstop flights to Anguilla from the United States, though there are codeshare connections via Seaborne Airlines through San Juan (SJU). Getting here is much faster if you fly to St. Maarten's Princess Juliana International SXM Airport and take a nearby ferry to Anguilla, about a half-hour ride away. Air Sunshine also flies several times a day from St. Thomas and San Juan, and Anguilla Air Services flies from St. Maarten and St. Barth. Tradewind Aviation flies in from San Juan. TransAnguilla provides charter services throughout the Caribbean.

LOCAL AIRLINE CONTACTS Air Sunshine. ☎ *800/327–8900* ⊕ *www. airsunshine.com.* **Anguilla Air Services.** ☎ *264/498–5922* ⊕ *www. anguillaairservices.com.* **Tradewind Aviation.** ☎ *800/376–7922, 203/267–3305* ⊕ *www.flytradewind.com.* **TransAnguilla Airways.** ☎ *264/497–8690* ⊕ *www.transanguilla.com.*

AIRPORT Clayton J. Lloyd International Airport. ☎ *264/498–4141* ⊕ *www.gov.ai/airport.php.*

BOAT AND FERRY TRAVEL

Public ferries run frequently between Anguilla and Marigot on French St. Martin. Boats leave from Blowing Point on Anguilla approximately every half hour from 7:30 am to 6:15 pm and from Marigot, St. Martin, every 45 minutes from 8 am to 7 pm. You pay a $23 departure tax before boarding ($5 for day-trippers coming through the Blowing Point terminal—but be sure to make this clear at the window where you pay), in addition to the $20 one-way fare. Fares require cash payment. Children under 12 years of age are $10. On very windy days the 20-minute trip can be fairly bouncy. The drive between the Marigot ferry terminal and the St. Maarten airport is vastly faster thanks to the causeway (bridge) across Simpson Bay lagoon. Some ferries operate between Blowing Point and Juliana Airport on the Dutch side of St. Maarten, with crossings four times daily. Fare is $55 one-way/$90 round-trip. Transfers by speedboat to Anguilla are available from a terminal right at the airport at a cost of about $75 per person (arranged directly with a company or through your Anguilla hotel). Private ferry companies listed below run six or more round-trips a day, coinciding with major flights, between Blowing Point and Princess Juliana airport in Dutch St. Maarten. On the St. Maarten side they will bring you right to the terminal in a van, or you can just walk across the parking lot. These trips are $65 one-way or $120 round-trip (cash only) and usually include departure taxes. There are also private charters available.

A late-night sea shuttle service, available to meet the late AA flight from Miami when it is operating, leaves St. Maarten for Anguilla at 11:30 pm. This sea shuttle (leaving Blowing Point Terminal at 10:30 pm) meets that daily American flight from Miami, which arrives at 9:55 pm. The ferry then takes you directly to Blowing Point in Anguilla. The trip costs $80 per adult and $40 per child.

CONTACTS Funtime Ferry. ☎ 866/978–8529 ⊕ www.funtimecharters.com. **GB Ferries.** ☎ 264/235–6205, 321/406–0414 in U.S. ⊕ www.gbferries.com. **Link Ferries.** ☎ 264/772–4901 ⊕ www.linkferry.com.

CAR TRAVEL

Although many of the rental cars on-island have the driver's side on the left as in North America, Anguillian roads are like those in the United Kingdom—driving is on the left side of the road. It's easy to get the hang of, but the roads can be rough, so be cautious, and observe the 30 mph (48 kph) speed limit. Roundabouts are probably the biggest driving obstacle for most. As you approach, give way to the vehicle on your right; once you're in the roundabout, you have the right of way.

Car Rentals: A temporary Anguilla driver's license is required to rent a car—you can get into real trouble if you're caught driving without one. You get it for $20 (good for three months) through any of the car-rental agencies at the time you pick up your car; you'll also need your valid driver's license from home. Rental rates start at about $45 to $55 per day, plus insurance.

CONTACTS Andy's Car Rental. ☎ 264/584–7010 ⊕ www.andyrentals. com. **Avis.** ⊠ Airport Rd. ☎ 264/497–2642 ⊕ www.avisanguilla. com. **Bryans Car Rental.** ☎ 264/497–6407 ⊕ www.bryanscarren-tals.com. **Triple K Car Rental/Hertz.** ⊠ Airport Rd. ☎ 264/497–2934 ⊕ www.hertz.com.

TAXI TRAVEL

Taxis are fairly expensive, so if you plan to explore many beaches and restaurants, it may be more cost-effective to rent a car. Taxi rates are regulated by the government, and there are fixed fares from point to point, listed in brochures the drivers should have handy and published in local guides. It's about $26 from the airport or $22 from Blowing Point Ferry to West End hotels. Posted rates are for one or two people; each additional passenger adds $5, and there is a $1 charge for each piece of luggage beyond the allotted two. You can also hire a taxi for a flat rate of $28 an hour. A surcharge of $4 applies to trips between 6 pm and midnight. After midnight it's $10. You'll always find taxis at the Blowing Point Ferry landing and the airport, but you'll need to call for hotel and restaurant pickups and arrange ahead with the driver who took you if you need a late-night return from a nightclub or bar.

CONTACTS Blowing Point Ferry Taxi Stand. ☎ 264/497–6089 ⊕ car-ibya.com/anguilla/taxis. **Maurice & Sons Exquisite Taxi Services.** ☎ 264/235–2676 ⊕ www.msexquisiteshuttle.com.

Health and Safety

Dengue, chikungunya, and zika have all been reported throughout the Caribbean. We recommend that you protect yourself from these mosquito-borne illnesses by keeping your skin covered and/or wearing mosquito repellent. The mosquitoes that transmit these viruses are as active by day as they are by night. Many locals swear by a product called "Mosquito Milk," a roll-on insect repellent available at many Caribbean pharmacies; it has a lemon-grass fragrance mosquitoes seem to hate.

Hotels and Resorts

Anguilla is known for its luxurious resorts and villas, but there are also some places that mere mortals can afford (and a few that are downright bargains).

Resorts. Anguilla is known for luxurious, expensive resorts.

Villas and rentals. Private villa rentals are becoming more common and are improving in quality of design and upkeep every season as development on the island accelerates. Condos, with full kitchens and multiple bedrooms, are great for families or for longer stays.

Hotel reviews have been shortened. For full information, visit Fodors.com.

What It Costs in U.S. Dollars			
$	$$	$$$	$$$$
RESTAURANTS			
under $12	$12–$20	$21–$30	over $30
HOTELS			
under $275	$275–$375	$376–$475	over $475

Visitor Information

CONTACTS Anguilla Tourist Board. ⊠ *Coronation Ave., The Valley* ☎ *264/497–2759* ⊕ *www.ivisitanguilla.com.*

◉ Sights

Exploring on Anguilla is mostly about checking out the spectacular beaches and resorts. The island has only a few roads. Locals are happy to provide directions, but using the readily available tourist map is the best idea. Visit the Anguilla Tourist Board, centrally located on Coronation Avenue in The Valley.

You can take a free, self-guided tour of the Anguilla Heritage Trail, consisting of 10 important historical sights that can be explored independently in any order. Wallblake House, in The Valley, is the main information center for the trail, or you can just look for the large boulders with descriptive plaques.

Bethel Methodist Church

HISTORIC SITE | Not far from Sandy Ground, this charming little church, which celebrated its 140th anniversary in 2018, is an

Sights

Bethel Methodist Church, 1

Heritage Museum Collection, 5

Island Harbour, 6

Old Factory, 4

Sandy Ground, 2

Wallblake House, 3

Restaurants

Blanchards, 7

Blanchards Beach Shack, 8

Cafe Celeste at Malliouhana, 9

da'Vida, 19

Dolce Vita Italian Beach Restaurant & Bar, 13

Elvis' Beach Bar, 15

English Rose Bar and Restaurant, 18

Hibernia Restaurant and Art Gallery, 21

Jacala Beach Restaurant, 10

Madeariman Reef Bar and Restaurant, 20

Mango's Seaside Grill, 4

Ocean Echo, 5

Picante, 3

Roy's Bayside Grill, 12

SandBar, 14

Sharky's, 2

Straw Hat, 6

Tasty's, 16

Tokyo Bay, 11

Trattoria Tramonto and Oasis Beach Bar, 1

Veya and Meze at Veya, 17

Hotels

Allamanda Beach Club, 15

Altamer, 1

Anguilla Great House Beach Resort, 12

Cap Juluca, 6

Caribella Beach Resort, 2

Carimar Beach Club, 8

CuisinArt Golf Resort and Spa, 11

Four Seasons Resort and Residences Anguilla, 5

Frangipani Beach Resort, 3

Malliouhana, An Auberge Resort, 9

Meads Bay Beach Villas, 4

Paradise Cove, 7

Serenity Cottages, 16

Shoal Bay Villas, 14

Turtle's Nest Beach Resort, 10

Zemi Beach House Hotel & Spa / Residences, 13

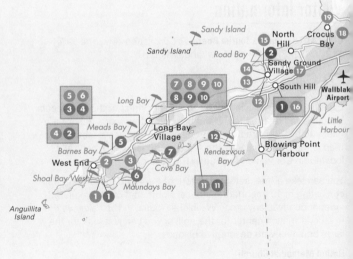

Anguilla

ATLANTIC
OCEAN

Little Scrub Island

Scrub Island

Upper Flats

Stoney Bay Marine Park

Grouper Bowl

Island Harbour

Captain's Bay

Shoal Bay

14 15

Scilly Cay

21

Heritage Museum
◇ Collection

Island
Harbour

13 20 16

Savannah Bay

Crocus Bay

Shoal Bay
Village

Katouche Bay

6

5

Mimi Bay

Sea Feathers Bay

THE VALLEY
The Quarter

Sandy Hill

Sandy Hill Bay

4

Long Salt Pond

3

Forest Bay

Ile Tintamarre

ST.
MARTIN

KEY	
1	*Exploring Sights*
1	*Restaurants*
1	*Hotels*
⛴	*Ferry*
⛱	*Beaches*
◥	*Dive Sights*

excellent example of skillful island stonework. It also has some colorful stained-glass windows. ⊠ *South Hill Village.*

Heritage Museum Collection

HISTORIC SITE | FAMILY | A remarkable opportunity to learn about Anguilla, this tiny museum (complete with gift shop) is painstakingly curated by Colville Petty. Old photographs and local records and artifacts trace the island's history over four millennia, from the days of the Arawaks. High points include historical documents of the Anguilla Revolution and photo albums chronicling island life, from devastating hurricanes to a visit from Queen Elizabeth in 1964. You can see examples of ancient pottery shards and stone tools along with fascinating photographs of the island in the early 20th century—many depicting the heaping and exporting of salt and the christening of schooners—and a complete set of beautiful postage stamps issued by Anguilla since 1967. ⊠ *East End at Pond Ground* ☎ *264/497–4092* 🖭 *$5.*

Island Harbour

LOCAL INTEREST | Anguillians have been fishing for centuries in the brightly painted, simple, handcrafted fishing boats that line the shore of the harbor. It's hard to believe, but skillful pilots take these little boats out to sea as far as 50 or 60 miles (80 or 100 km). Late afternoon is the best time to see the day's catch, and there are a couple of good, laid-back beach restaurants here.
■ **TIP→ Scilly Cay, the classic little offshore restaurant offering sublime lobster and Eudoxie Wallace's knockout rum punches, is still hoping to reopen following Hurricane Irma. They have already completed some rebuilding: stay tuned.** ⊠ *Island Harbor Rd.*

Old Factory

HISTORIC SITE | For many years the cotton grown on Anguilla and exported to England was processed in this beautiful historic building. Later it was a general store, and now it's the home of Sotheby's Real Estate. There is a small art gallery on the lower level in an old stone cellar featuring works by the renowned Caribbean plein-air Impressionist artist, Sir Roland Richardson. ⊠ *Government Corner, The Valley* ☎ *264/498–0123* ⊕ *www.anguilla-beaches.com/anguilla-history-heritage-trail.html* 🖭 *Free.*

Sandy Ground

BEACH—SIGHT | Almost everyone who comes to Anguilla stops by this central beach, home to several popular open-air bars and restaurants, as well as boat-rental operations. This is where you catch the ferry for tiny Sandy Island, 2 miles (3 km) offshore. ☎ *264/476–6534* ⊕ *www.mysandyisland.com.*

Wallblake House

HISTORIC SITE | Anguilla's only surviving plantation house, Wallblake House was built in 1787 by Will Blake (Wallblake is probably a corruption of his name). The place is associated with many a tale involving murder, high living, and the French invasion in 1796. On the grounds are an ancient vaulted stone cistern and an outbuilding called the Bakery, which wasn't used for making bread at all but for baking turkeys and hams. You can visit the thoroughly and thoughtfully restored house and grounds only on a guided tour, usually offered two days a week. It's also the information center for the Anguilla Heritage Trail. Call for tour reservations. ⊠ *Wallblake Rd., The Valley* ☎ *264/497–6613* ⊕ *www.wallblake.ai* ⊠ *Free.*

🏝 Beaches

Anguilla's beaches are among the best and most beautiful in the Caribbean. You can find long, deserted stretches suitable for sunset walks and beaches lined with lively bars and restaurants—all surrounded by crystal-clear warm waters in several shades of turquoise. The sea is calmest at 2½-mile-long (4-km-long) Rendezvous Bay, where gentle breezes tempt sailors. But Shoal Bay (East) is the quintessential Caribbean beach. The white sand is so soft and abundant that it pools around your ankles. Cove Bay and Maundays Bay also rank among the island's best beaches. Maundays is the location of the island's famous resort Cap Juluca. Meads Bay's arc is dominated by the tony Four Seasons Resort, and smaller Cove Bay is just a walk away. Anguilla doesn't permit topless sunbathing.

NORTHEAST COAST

Captain's Bay

BEACH—SIGHT | On the north coast just before the eastern tip of the island, this quarter-mile stretch of perfect white sand is bounded by a rocky shoreline where Atlantic waves crash. If you make the tough, four-wheel-drive-only trip along the dirt road that leads to the northeastern end of the island toward Junk's Hole, you'll be rewarded with peaceful isolation. The surf here slaps the sands with a vengeance, and the undertow is strong—so wading is the safest water sport. **Amenities:** none. **Best for:** solitude.

Island Harbour

BEACH—SIGHT | For centuries Anguillians have ventured from these sands in colorful handmade fishing boats. Mostly calm waters are surrounded by a slender beach—good sightseeing, but not much for swimming or lounging. But there are a couple of good restaurants (Hibernia, offering dinner, and Falcon Nest, a casual spot for lunch and dinner). This area is also the departure point for a three-minute boat ride to Scilly Cay, where a thatched beach bar serves seafood. Just hail the restaurant's free boat and plan to spend most of the day (the all-inclusive lunch—Wednesday and Sunday only—starts at $40 and is worth the price). **Amenities:** food and drink; toilets. **Best for:** partiers.

NORTHWEST COAST

Little Bay

BEACH—SIGHT | On the north coast, not far from The Valley, this small gray-sand beach is a favored spot for snorkeling and night dives. It's essentially accessible only by water, as it's backed by sheer cliffs lined with agave and creeping vines. The easiest way to get here is a five-minute boat ride from Crocus Bay (about $10 round-trip). There are no amenities, so take some snacks with you. The only way to access the beach from the road is to clamber down the cliffs by rope to explore the caves and surrounding reef—for young, agile, and experienced climbers only. Do not leave personal items in cars parked here, because theft can be a problem. **Amenities:** none. **Best for:** snorkeling.

Road Bay (*Sandy Ground*)

BEACH—SIGHT | The big pier here is where the cargo ships dock, but so do some impressive yachts, sailboats, and fishing boats. The brown-sugar sand is home to terrific restaurants that hop from day through dawn, including Veya, Roy's Bayside Grille, Dolce Vita, Sand Bar, the Pumphouse, and Elvis', the quintessential (and rather famous) beach bar. There are all kinds of boat charters available here. The snorkeling isn't very good, but the sunset vistas are glorious, especially with a rum punch in your hand. **Amenities:** food and drink. **Best for:** sunset.

Sandy Island

BEACH—SIGHT | A popular day trip, tiny Sandy Island shelters a pretty lagoon nestled in coral reefs about 2 miles (3 km) from Road Bay, with a restaurant that serves lunch and great islandy cocktails. From November through August you can take the *Happiness* sea shuttle from Sandy Ground ($10 round-trip). There is mooring for yachts and larger sailboats. Small boats can come right in the channel. ■ TIP→ **The reef is great for snorkeling. Amenities:** food and drink. **Best for:** partiers; snorkeling; swimming. ⊕ *www. mysandyisland.com*.

★ Shoal Bay

BEACH—SIGHT | FAMILY | Anchored by seagrape and coconut trees, the 2-mile (3-km) powdered-sugar strand at Shoal Bay (not to be confused with Shoal Bay West, at the other end of the island) is one of the world's prettiest beaches. You can park free at any of the restaurants, including Elodia's, Madeariman's, or Gwen's

Reggae Bar & Grill, most of which either rent or provide chairs and umbrellas for patrons for about $20 a day per person. There is plenty of room to stretch out in relative privacy, or you can bar-hop or take a ride on Junior's Glass Bottom Boat. The relatively broad beach has shallow water that is usually gentle, making this a great family beach; a coral reef not far from the shore is a wonderful snorkeling spot. Sunsets over the water are spectacular. **Amenities:** food and drink. **Best for:** sunset; swimming; walking.

SOUTHEAST COAST
Sandy Hill
BEACH—SIGHT | You can park anywhere along the dirt road to Sea Feathers Bay to visit this popular fishing center. What's good for the fishermen is also good for snorkelers, with a coral reef right near the shore. But the beach here is not much of a lounging spot. The sand is too narrow and rocky. However, for those with creative culinary skills, it's a great place to buy lobsters and fish fresh from local waters in the afternoon. **Amenities:** food and drink. **Best for:** snorkeling; walking.

SOUTHWEST COAST
★ Maundays Bay
BEACH—SIGHT | The dazzling, platinum-white mile-long beach is especially great for swimming and long beach walks. It's no wonder that Cap Juluca, one of Anguilla's premier resorts, chose this as its location. Public parking is straight ahead at the end of the road near Cap Juluca's Pimms restaurant. You can have lunch or dinner here (be prepared for the cost) or, depending on the season, book a massage in one of the beachside tents. **Amenities:** food and drink; parking (no fee); toilets. **Best for:** partiers; swimming; walking.

★ Meads Bay
BEACH—SIGHT | FAMILY | Arguably Anguilla's premier beach, Meads Bay is home to many of the island's top resorts (Malliouhana, Four Seasons) and a dozen fine restaurants. Megayachts moor offshore. The powder-soft champagne sand is great for a long walk and is as beautiful now as it has ever been. Park at any of the restaurants, and plan for lunch. Several of the restaurants offer chaises for patrons. **Amenities:** food and drink; parking (no fee); toilets. **Best for:** partiers; swimming; walking.

Rendezvous Bay
BEACH—SIGHT | FAMILY | Follow the signs to Anguilla Great House for public parking at this broad swath of pearl-white sand that is some 1½ miles (2½ km) long. The beach is lapped by calm, bluer-than-blue water and a postcard-worthy view of St. Martin. The expansive crescent is home to three resorts; stop in for a drink or

a meal at one, or rent a chair and umbrella at one of the kiosks. Don't miss the daylong party at the tree-house Dune Preserve, where Bankie Banx, Anguilla's most famous musician, presides. (Jimmy Buffett recorded a concert there several years back, too.) **Amenities:** food and drink; parking (no fee); toilets. **Best for:** partiers; swimming; walking.

Shoal Bay West

BEACH—SIGHT | This glittering bay bordered by mangroves and seagrapes is a lovely place to spend the day. The 1-mile-long (1½-km-long) beach offers sublime tranquility with coral reefs for snorkeling not too far from shore. Hollywood notables are often sighted here and occasionally an ex-president. Punctuate your day with lunch or dinner at beachside Trattoria Tramonto and you can use their chairs and umbrellas. Reach the beach by taking the main road to the West End and bearing left at the fork, then continuing to the end. Note that similarly named Shoal Bay is a separate beach on a different part of the island. **Amenities:** food and drink; parking (no fee); toilets. **Best for:** solitude; swimming; walking.

🍴 Restaurants

Despite its small size, Anguilla has around 70 restaurants: stylish temples of haute cuisine; classic, barefoot beachfront grills; roadside barbecue stands; food vans; and casual cafés. Many have breeze-swept terraces for dining under the stars. Call ahead—in winter to make a reservation and in late summer and fall to confirm whether the place is open. Anguillian restaurant meals are leisurely events, and service often has a relaxed pace, so settle in and enjoy. Most restaurant owners are actively and conspicuously present, especially at dinner.

What to Wear: During the day, casual clothes are widely accepted: shorts will be fine, but don't wear bathing suits and cover-ups unless you're at a beach bar. In the evening, shorts are okay at the extremely casual eateries. Elsewhere, women wear sundresses or nice casual slacks; men will be fine in short-sleeve shirts and casual pants or nice shorts. Some hotel restaurants are slightly more formal, but that just means long pants for men.

★ Blanchards

$$$$ | **ECLECTIC** | Creative cuisine, an upscale atmosphere, attentive service, and an excellent wine cellar please the star-studded crowd at Blanchard's, one of the best restaurants in the Caribbean. Ever changing but always good, the contemporary menu wins over even the most sophisticated palates. **Known for:** the owners' book, "A Trip To The Beach," which has motivated many to visit; exquisite presentation; fine dining. $ *Average main: $43* ⊠ *Long Bay Village* ☎ *264/497–6100* ⊕ *www.blanchardsrestaurant.com* ⊗ *Closed Sun. No lunch.*

Blanchards Beach Shack

$$ | **AMERICAN** | **FAMILY** | This spin-off on the sands of Meads Bay Beach is the perfect antidote to high restaurant prices. Right next to Blanchards, this chartreuse-and-turquoise cottage serves delicious lunches and dinners of lobster rolls, all-natural burgers, tacos, and terrific salads and sandwiches, and there are lots of choices for children and vegetarians. **Known for:** beach food with a twist; generous portions; "the wait" from 12:30 on. $ *Average main: $12* ⊠ *Long Bay Village* ☎ *264/498–6100* ⊕ *www. blanchardsrestaurant.com* ⊗ *Closed Sun.–Wed. Oct. 1–Nov. 1, and Aug. 22–Aug. 31.*

★ Cafe Celeste at Malliouhana

$$$$ | **ECLECTIC** | The romantic open-air setting of Cafe Celeste on a promontory overlooking Meads Bay sets the stage for a memorable meal. The café's dishes are inspired by Mediterranean seafaring cultures, including pistou, a simple soup of vegetables and pesto, sautéed clams and mussels, tender charred octopus, and more. **Known for:** Malli sunset cocktails; citrus-rosemary lamb chops; goat cheese crème brûlée. $ *Average main: $35* ⊠ *Meads Bay, Long Bay Village* ☎ *264/497–6111* ⊕ *aubergeresorts.com/ malliouhana/dine/cafe-celeste* ⊗ *Closed Aug. 28–Oct. 28* ▭ *No credit cards.*

da'Vida

$$$$ | **CARIBBEAN** | **FAMILY** | You could spend the whole day dining, drinking, snorkeling, kayaking, shopping, and lounging on the comfortable chairs at this beautifully designed resort, restaurant, and club on exquisite Crocus Bay. Picnic at the Beach Grill (burgers, hot dogs, wraps, salads) or head inside the main building for dumplings, soups, pastas, and pizzas. **Known for:** perfect beach drinks like rum punch and piña colada; salads that are a meal unto themselves; pizzas with extra toppings. $ *Average main: $38* ⊠ *Crocus Bay* ☎ *264/498–5433* ⊕ *www.davidaanguilla.com* ⊗ *Closed Mon.*

Dolce Vita Italian Beach Restaurant & Bar

$$$$ | **ITALIAN** | Serious Italian cuisine and warm and attentive service are provided in a romantic beachside pavilion in Sandy Ground. It all starts with meticulously sourced seafood and freshly made pasta, which stars in classic lasagna, Gorgonzola-wrapped gnocchi, and a meatless eggplant parmigiana. **Known for:** red snapper caught the day it is served; swordfish carpaccio; lobster pasta.

$ *Average main: $45* ✉ *Sandy Ground Village* ☎ *264/497–8668* ⊗ *Closed Sun. and Sept.–mid-Oct. No lunch.*

★ Elvis' Beach Bar

$$ | **MODERN AMERICAN** | One of the most famous beach restaurants in the Caribbean, Elvis' is a hub of nightlife on the island, catering to all kinds of visitors and Hollywood A-listers. The bar is actually a boat; you can sit around it or with your feet in the sand under umbrella-covered tables on the beach. **Known for:** people-watching; big screen TVs with sports on; Mexican food and potent drinks. $ *Average main: $18* ✉ *Northern End, Sandy Ground beach* ☎ *264/498–0101* ⊕ *elvisbeachbar.com.*

English Rose Bar and Restaurant

$$ | **CARIBBEAN** | This middle-of-The-Valley landmark serves generous portions at small prices, and the selection is large for a small restaurant. With such a variety and low prices, lunchtime finds the neighborhood hangout packed with locals. **Known for:** conveniently located in The Valley, next to Peoples Market; generous portions at reasonable prices; people-watching. $ *Average main: $14* ✉ *Carter Rey Blvd., The Valley* ☎ *264/497–5353* ⊗ *Closed Sun.*

★ Hibernia Restaurant and Art Gallery

$$$$ | **ECLECTIC** | Creative dishes are served in this wood-beam cottage restaurant overlooking the water at Anguilla's eastern end. The lovely Zen garden has been redesigned with a small waterfall and stone artifacts from Bali, and the intimate dining room (only nine tables) has been updated, also. **Known for:** eclectic dining; can't-miss smoked fish appetizer; lavender and coconut ice cream meringue cake. $ *Average main: $36* ✉ *Harbor Ridge Dr., Island Harbour* ☎ *264/497–4290* ⊕ *www.hiberniarestaurant.com* ⊗ *Closed Mon. and mid-July–Nov.*

★ Jacala Beach Restaurant

$$$ | **FRENCH** | On beautiful Meads Bay, this restaurant continues to receive raves, with even Martha Stewart dubbing it her "new favorite Caribbean restaurant." Chef Alain (named one of the Caribbean's top 25 chefs) and maître d' Jacques (from the "old" Malliouhana) have created a lovely open-air restaurant that turns out carefully prepared and nicely presented French food accompanied by good wines and personal attention. A delicious starter terrine of feta and grilled vegetables is infused with pesto. **Known for:** best-in-the-Caribbean reputation; out-of-this-world tuna carpaccio; filet mignon cooked to perfection. $ *Average main: $30* ✉ *Long Bay Village* ☎ *264/498–5888* ⊗ *Closed Mon. and Tues. and Aug. and Sept.*

Straw Hat's outdoor patio on Forest Bay is a great place to catch the sunset.

Madeariman Reef Bar and Restaurant

$$ | BRASSERIE | This casual, feet-in-the-sand bistro right on busy, beautiful Shoal Bay is open for breakfast, lunch, and dinner. The soups, salads, and simple grills here are served in generous portions with a bit of French flair, and the pizza is cooked in a stone oven. **Known for:** prime location on Shoal Bay; pizza; huge variety of seafood. $ *Average main: $14* ⊠ *Shoal Bay Village* ☎ *264/498–5888.*

Mango's Seaside Grill

$$$$ | SEAFOOD | FAMILY | Sparkling-fresh fish specialties have starring roles here. Light and healthy choices include spicy grilled whole snapper and Cruzan rum–barbecued chicken, while the warm apple tart and coconut cheesecake are worth a splurge. **Known for:** laid-back but high-end atmosphere; Anguillian lobster; Anguilla's only banana splits. $ *Average main: $36* ⊠ *Barnes Bay* ☎ *264/497–6479* ⊕ *www.mangosseasidegrill.com* ⊗ *Closed Tues. and Aug. and Sept.*

Ocean Echo

$$$$ | CARIBBEAN | FAMILY | It's nonstop every day from lunch until late at this relaxed and friendly restaurant, great for salads, burgers, grills, pasta, and fresh fish. Heartier appetites will enjoy the ribs and steaks. **Known for:** the "Rumzie," Anguilla's rum punch; club sandwiches; lobster salad. $ *Average main: $35* ⊠ *Long Bay Village* ☎ *264/498–5454* ⊕ *www.oceanechoanguilla.com.*

Picante

$$$ | **MEXICAN** | **FAMILY** | This casual, wildly popular bright-red roadside Caribbean *taquería,* opened by a young California couple, serves huge, tasty burritos with a choice of fillings, fresh warm tortilla chips with first-rate guacamole, huge (and fresh) taco salads, seafood enchiladas, chipotle ribs, and tequila-lime chicken grilled under a brick. Passion-fruit margaritas are a must, and there are some serious tequila options. **Known for:** passion-fruit margarita; chicken tacos; picnic-table seating. $ *Average main: $21* ✉ *West End Rd., West End Village* ☎ *264/498–1616* ⊕ *www.picante-restaurant-anguilla.com* ✪ *Closed Tues. and mid-Aug.–Nov. 1. No lunch.*

Roy's Bayside Grill

$$$ | **CARIBBEAN** | **FAMILY** | Roy's is comfort food heaven, whether you crave red snapper fish-and-chips or a hamburger with all the fixings. Come any time of day for good cooking and a friendly vibe. **Known for:** home-style cooking; Angus burger with great onion rings; Anguillian johnnycakes. $ *Average main: $27* ✉ *Road Bay, Sandy Ground Village* ☎ *264/497–2470* ⊕ *www.roysbayside-grill.com.*

SandBar

$$ | **ECLECTIC** | Tasty and shareable small plates, a friendly beach vibe, and gorgeous sunsets are on offer here, as are cool music, gentle prices, a hammock on the beach, and potent tropical cocktails. The menu changes seasonally, but it always features tapas brought to a new level, usually traditional foods prepared in unconventional ways. **Known for:** big tapas plates; local snapper; fun food and reasonable prices. $ *Average main: $13* ✉ *Sandy Ground Village* ☎ *264/498–0171.*

Sharky's

$$$ | **CARIBBEAN** | A not-to-be-missed restaurant where Caribbean flavors steal the show, Sharky's is a result of Chef Lowell Hodge's perfectionism. He does a few things here and does them well, as a usually full house well attests ("house," by the way, is an operative word—you'll dine on the front porch of a private home). **Known for:** Caribbean dishes; high-end dining for a fraction of the price; few menu items but all are hits. $ *Average main: $24* ✉ *Rte. 1 West End Village and Albert Hughes Dr.* ✛ *Just past the gas station* ☎ *264/729-0059* ▭ *No credit cards.*

★ Straw Hat

$$$$ | **ECLECTIC** | **FAMILY** | Charming owners, a gorgeous oceanfront location, sophisticated and original food, and friendly service are why this stylish restaurant has been in business since the mid-1990s. Whether for breakfast, lunch, or dinner, you will find

appealing, tasty, and fresh choices to mix up or share. **Known for:** ahi tuna bites; spicy mahi sandwich; Anguilla's only "real" bagel. $ *Average main: $32* ✉ *Frangipani Beach Club, Long Bay Village* ☎ *264/497–8300* ⊕ *www.strawhat.com* ⊗ *Closed Sept. and Oct.*

Tasty's

$$$ | **CARIBBEAN** | **FAMILY** | Once your eyes adjust to the kiwi, lilac, and coral color scheme, you'll find that breakfast, lunch, tapas, or dinner at Tasty's is, well, very tasty. It's open all day, so if you land midafternoon starving, head here—it's just a few minutes' drive from the airport or the ferry terminal. **Known for:** classic Caribbean with a creole edge; coconut-crusted parrotfish in banana rum sauce; warm goat cheese salad. $ *Average main: $26* ✉ *Main Rd., South Hill Village* ☎ *264/584–2737* ⊗ *Closed Thurs.*

★ Tokyo Bay

$$$$ | **SUSHI** | **FAMILY** | This sophisticated sushi and teppanyaki restaurant, dramatically lit and perched at the top of CuisinArt's spa building, owes its raves to its chef from Nobu in London. Chances are you will find local chefs and other restaurant people here on their night out. **Known for:** sushi and teppanyaki; teriyaki salmon with Okinawa sweet potato puree; sake bar. $ *Average main: $42* ✉ *CuisinArt Golf Resort and Spa, Rendezvous Bay* ☎ *264/498–2000* ⊕ *www.cuisinartresort.com* ⊗ *Closed Tues. No lunch.*

Trattoria Tramonto and Oasis Beach Bar

$$$ | **ITALIAN** | **FAMILY** | The island's beloved beachfront Italian restaurant features a dual (or dueling) serenade of soft jazz on the sound system and gently lapping waves a few feet away. Pastas are homemade and served in a dozen ways. **Known for:** classic Italian dining next to the sea; relaxing tropical ambience; celebrity sightings. $ *Average main: $27* ✉ *Shoal Bay Village* ☎ *264/497–8819* ⊕ *www.trattoriatramonto.com* ⊗ *Closed Mon. and Aug.–Oct.*

★ Veya and Meze at Veya

$$$$ | **ECLECTIC** | On the suavely minimalist four-sided verandah, stylishly appointed tables glow with flickering candlelight from sea urchin–shape porcelain votive holders. Chic patrons mingle and sip mojitos to the purr of soft jazz in a lively lounge. **Known for:** Veya sparklers; Moroccan shrimp "cigars"; live music nightly. $ *Average main: $44* ✉ *Sandy Ground Village* ☎ *264/498–8392* ⊕ *www.veya-axa.com* ⊗ *Closed Sun. and Sept.–mid-Oct. Closed Sat. in June–Aug. and in late Oct. No lunch.*

🛏 Hotels

Tourism on Anguilla is newer than some Caribbean islands—most development didn't begin until the early 1980s. The lack of native topography and, indeed, vegetation, and the blindingly white expanses of beach have inspired building designs of some interest; architecture buffs might have fun trying to name some of the most surprising examples. Inspiration largely comes from the Mediterranean: the Greek Islands, Morocco, and Spain, with some Miami-style art deco thrown into the mixture.

Anguilla accommodations basically fall into two categories: grand resorts and luxury resort-villas, or low-key, simple, locally owned apartments and small beachfront complexes. The former can be surprisingly expensive, the latter surprisingly reasonable. In the middle are some condo-type options, with full kitchens and multiple bedrooms, which are great for families or for longer stays. Private villa rentals are becoming more common and are increasing in number and quality of design and upkeep every season as development on the island accelerates.

A good phone chat or email exchange with the management of any property is a good idea, as units within the same complex can vary greatly in layout, accessibility, distance to the beach, and view. When calling to reserve a room, ask about special discount packages, especially in spring and summer. Most hotels include continental breakfast in the price, and many have meal-plan options. But keep in mind that Anguilla is home to dozens of excellent restaurants before you lock yourself into an expensive meal plan that you may not be able to change. All hotels charge a 10% tax, a $1 per room/per day tourism marketing levy, and—in most cases—an additional 10% service charge. A few properties include these charges in the published rates, so check carefully when evaluating prices.

PRIVATE VILLAS AND CONDOS
The tourist office publishes an annual *Anguilla Travel Planner* with informative listings of available vacation apartment rentals.

RENTAL CONTACTS
Ani Private Resorts
Ani offers private resorts in several countries; in Anguilla, they offer two stunning cliffside villas for up to 24 guests, delivering breathtaking views and total luxury to families or groups looking for pampering. Included in the rental are private boat transfers from St. Martin, rental car, a full-service team (concierge, butler, chef, housekeepers), breakfast, and all beverages. A tennis court, bikes, fitness room, pool, cliffside hot tubs, and playrooms mean

CuisinArt Golf Resort and Spa is a family-friendly resort on Rendezvous Bay.

you don't have to leave except for the beach. (Tennis pros, spa services, trainers, and guides are available on demand.) There is room for 100 guests for a party or wedding on the dramatic and romantic promontory. Promotions can include unlimited golf at the CuisinArt course. ⊠ *Little Bay* ☎ *718/577–1188* ⊕ *www.anivillas. com.*

Kishti Villa Collection

This group of stunning four- and five-bedroom villas fuses Eastern and Western aesthetics. The name, from the Urdu for "canoe," expresses a mystic sense of being in tune with nature and the lords of creation. Appointed with lovely Asian artifacts, villas have huge windows and gorgeous views, giving the sense of actually being at sea. While rates are high, attention is paid to every detail, and everything from a full staff, house manager, chef, and sports equipment is included. This remains a terrific choice for destination weddings and other large family gatherings. ⊠ *Long Bay Village* ☎ *264/235–2110* ⊕ *www.villakishticollection.com.*

Ricketts Luxury Properties

The Ricketts, longtime Anguilla residents, manage lovely luxury properties as well as a selection of less expensive villas. ☎ *264/497–6049* ⊕ *www.rickettsluxury.com.*

RECOMMENDED HOTELS AND RESORTS

Allamanda Beach Club

$ | RENTAL | FAMILY | Youthful, active couples from around the globe happily fill this quiet, casual, three-story, white-stucco building hidden in a palm grove a short walk from the beach, opting for location and price over luxury. **Pros:** easy on the pocketbook; young crowd; close to beach. **Cons:** location requires a car; rooms are pleasant but not fancy; this part of Shoal Bay has suffered recent beach erosion. $ *Rooms from: $169* ⊠ *The Valley* ☎ *264/497–5217, 305/396–4472* ⊕ *www.allamanda.ai* ☽ *Closed Sept.* ⇄ *20 units* ¶❶ *No meals.*

Altamer

$$$$ | RENTAL | FAMILY | Architect Myron Goldfinger's geometric symphony of floor-to-ceiling windows, cantilevered walls, and curvaceous floating staircases set on a white-sand private beach is fit for any celebrity (or CEO)—as is the price tag. **Pros:** stunning decor and beautiful architectural design; outstanding luxury and service; great for big groups. **Cons:** a bit out of the way; you'll very likely need a big group to split the price tag. $ *Rooms from: $22,500* ⊠ *Rte. 1, Shoal Bay Village* ☎ *800/475–9233* ⊕ *www. altamer.com* ⇄ *5 villas* ¶❶ *Some meals.*

Anguilla Great House Beach Resort

$ | RESORT | FAMILY | These traditional West Indian–style bungalows are strung along one of Anguilla's longest beaches. **Pros:** real, old-school Caribbean; right on the gorgeous beach; good prices. **Cons:** very simple rooms; spotty Internet, if any; not exquisite or luxurious, which many seek in Anguilla. $ *Rooms from: $210* ⊠ *Rendezvous Bay* ☎ *264/497–6061, 800/583–9247* ⊕ *www. anguillagreathouse.com* ⇄ *31 rooms* ¶❶ *Some meals.*

★ Cap Juluca

$$$$ | RESORT | FAMILY | Strung along 179 acres of breathtaking Maundays Bay, these romantic, domed, Moorish-style villas are a long-time Anguilla favorite, thanks to a caring staff, great sports facilities, and plenty of privacy and comfort. **Pros:** miles of talcum-soft sand; impeccable, warm service; renovated after Hurricane Irma. **Cons:** may be booked well in advance; comparatively high rates. $ *Rooms from: $875* ⊠ *Maunday's Bay* ☎ *264/497–6666, 264/497–6779 reservations* ⊕ *www.belmond. com/hotels/caribbean/anguilla/belmond-cap-juluca* ⇄ *108 rooms* ¶❶ *Some meals.*

Caribella Beach Resort

$$$$ | RENTAL | These spacious Mediterranean-style villas on the broad sands of Barnes Bay are a good deal at the much-discounted weekly rate. **Pros:** huge amount of space for the cost; beautiful views from huge balconies; the beach makes everything just fine. **Cons:** basic decor; minimum stays in high season, December, and February; some bedrooms do not have air-conditioning. $ *Rooms from: $495* ⊠ *Barnes Bay* ☎ *800/969–8002* ⊕ *www.lambertventures.com* ⇄ *6 units* ¶❶ *No meals.*

Carimar Beach Club

$$$ | **RENTAL** | **FAMILY** | Recently renovated, this horseshoe of bougainvillea-draped Mediterranean-style buildings on beautiful Meads Bay has the look of a Sun Belt condo. **Pros:** great value; easy walk to restaurants and spa; excellent beach location. **Cons:** no pool or restaurant; air-conditioning only in bedrooms; not much privacy in the courtyard. ⑤ *Rooms from: $310* ✉ *Meads Bay, West End Village* ☎ *264/497–6881, 866/270–3764* ⊕ *www.carimar.com* ⊗ *Closed Sept.–mid-Oct.* ⤴ *24 apartments* ⦿ *Some meals.*

★ CuisinArt Golf Resort and Spa

$$$$ | **RESORT** | **FAMILY** | Anguilla's best family-friendly full-service resort has it all: miles of stunning beach, world-class golf, a gorgeous spa and health club, top dining, sports galore, and a creative outdoor play area for kids. **Pros:** family-friendly; great spa, sports, and on-site restaurants; gorgeous beach and gardens. **Cons:** food service can be slow; pool area can get noisy; property can be busy. ⑤ *Rooms from: $995* ✉ *Rendezvous Bay* ☎ *264/498–2000, 800/943–3210* ⊕ *www.cuisinartresort.com* ⊗ *Closed Sept. and Oct.* ⤴ *108 units* ⦿ *Some meals.*

★ Four Seasons Resort and Residences Anguilla

$$$$ | **RESORT** | **FAMILY** | On a promontory over 3,200 feet of pearly sand on Barnes Bay, this showpiece (formerly the Viceroy) wows international sophisticates. **Pros:** state-of-the-art luxury; cutting-edge contemporary design; spacious rooms. **Cons:** international rather than Caribbean feel; very large resort; expensive. ⑤ *Rooms from: $800* ✉ *Barnes Bay, West End Village* ☎ *800/819–5053 in U.S.* ⊕ *www.fourseasons.com* ⊗ *Closed Sept.* ⤴ *166 units* ⦿ *Free breakfast.*

Frangipani Beach Resort

$$$ | **RESORT** | **FAMILY** | Perfect for independent travelers, this flamingo-pink Mediterranean-style property perches on the beautiful champagne sands of Meads Bay. The property feels more like a condo than a resort, but there are kayaks, paddleboats, and a Hobie Cat, as well as a tennis court and two swimming pools. **Pros:** great beach; good location for restaurants and resort-hopping; first-rate on-site restaurant. **Cons:** some rooms lack a view; more like a condo than a resort; you will not want to leave. ⑤ *Rooms from: $450* ✉ *Meads Bay, West End Village* ☎ *264/497–6442, 877/593–8988* ⊕ *www.frangipaniresort.com* ⊗ *Closed Sept. and Oct.* ⤴ *19 rooms* ⦿ *Free breakfast.*

★ Malliouhana, An Auberge Resort

$$$ | **RESORT** | This classic luxury hotel perched cliffside over beautiful Meads Bay beach is a fancifully modern beach paradise. **Pros:** great location on Meads Bay; friendly and attentive service;

spacious rooms and bathrooms. **Cons:** lots of stairs and no elevators; property takes a fair amount of walking to get around; car necessary to explore the island (if you want to). $ *Rooms from: $400* ⊠ *Meads Bay* ☎ *264/497–6111* ⊕ *aubergeresorts.com/malliouhana* ☉ *Closed late Aug.–late Oct.* ☞ *46 rooms* ❏ *Free breakfast.*

Meads Bay Beach Villas

$$$$ | **RENTAL** | **FAMILY** | These gorgeous one-, two-, and three-bedroom villas right on Meads Bay have a cult following, so it can be hard to book them, but if you score a stay here, you'll understand why. **Pros:** big private apartments; beautiful beach; private plunge pools. **Cons:** more condo than hotel in terms of service; very busy resort but service still remains excellent; if you like complaining, you may get bored—this is a top-notch resort. $ *Rooms from: $575* ⊠ *Meads Bay Rd., West End Village* ☎ *267/685–6495* ⊕ *www.meadsbaybeachvillas.com* ☞ *4 villas* ❏ *No meals.*

Paradise Cove

$$ | **RENTAL** | **FAMILY** | Located 500 yards away from Cove Beach, this simple complex of huge, reasonably priced studios and one- and two-bedroom apartments has two whirlpools, a large pool, and tranquil tropical gardens where you can pluck fresh guavas for breakfast. **Pros:** reasonable rates for a lot of space; great pool; lovely gardens. **Cons:** 500 yards is far from the beach; bland decor; not luxury accommodations, which some might expect. $ *Rooms from: $375* ⊠ *Cove Bay* ☎ *264/497–6603 reservations* ☞ *29 units* ❏ *No meals.*

Serenity Cottages

$$ | **RENTAL** | **FAMILY** | Despite the name, these aren't cottages but large, fully equipped, and relatively affordable one- and two-bedroom apartments (and studios created from them) in a small complex set in a lush garden at the far end of glorious Shoal Bay Beach. **Pros:** quiet end of beach with snorkeling outside the door; weeklong packages; two convenient restaurants. **Cons:** no pool; more condo than hotel in terms of staff; location requires a car and extra time to drive to the West End. $ *Rooms from: $325* ⊠ *Shoal Bay Village* ☎ *264/497–3328* ⊕ *www.serenity.ai* ☉ *Closed Sept.* ☞ *10 units* ❏ *No meals.*

Shoal Bay Villas

$$$ | **RENTAL** | **FAMILY** | In this old-style property on Shoal Bay's incredible 2-mile (3-km) beach, studios and one- and two-bedroom apartments all have balconies over the water. **Pros:** friendly and casual; full kitchens; beachfront. **Cons:** rather basic; you'll want a car; luxury touches are lacking. $ *Rooms from: $385* ⊠ *Shoal Bay*

Village 📞 *264/497–2051* ⊕ *www.sbvillas.ai* ⊗ *Closed Aug. 30–Oct. 24* 🛏 *12 units* 🍽 *No meals.*

Turtle's Nest Beach Resort

$$ | RENTAL | FAMILY | This complex of studios and one- to three-bedroom oceanfront condos is right on Meads Bay Beach, with some of the island's best restaurants a sandy stroll away. **Pros:** beachfront; huge apartments; well-kept grounds and pool. **Cons:** no elevator, so fourth-floor units are a climb (but have great views); seven-night minimum stay in high season; may be busy in high season. ⑤ *Rooms from: $374* ✉ *Meads Bay, West End Village* 📞 *264/497–7979* ⊕ *www.turtlesnestbeachresort.com* 🛏 *29 units* 🍽 *No meals.*

Zemi Beach House Hotel & Spa / Residences

$$$$ | RESORT | This new luxury resort is on a gorgeous, 400-foot stretch of Shoal Bay East's white-sand beach. **Pros:** fabulous beach location; desirable amenities such as a lap pool, spa, and a rum and cigar room; beautiful boutique property. **Cons:** need a car to get around the island; during busiest weeks restaurant service may be less than perfect. ⑤ *Rooms from: $699* ✉ *Shoal Bay Village* 📞 *264/584–0001* ⊕ *www.zemibeach.com* 🛏 *69 rooms* 🍽 *No meals.*

🍸 Nightlife

In late February or early March, on the first full moon before Easter, reggae star and impresario Bankie Banx stages Moonsplash, a three-day music festival that showcases local and imported talent. Anguilla Day's boat races, in May, are the most important sporting event of the year. At the end of July, the Anguilla Summer Festival has boat races by day and Carnival parades, calypso competitions, and parties at night. Some years bring a jazz festival.

Nightlife action doesn't really start until 11 and runs late into the night. Be aware that taxis are not readily available then. If you plan to take a cab back to your lodging at the end of the night, make arrangements in advance with the driver who brings you or with your hotel concierge.

Dune Preserve

MUSIC CLUBS | There is music most nights at the funky driftwood-fabricated home of reggae star Bankie Banx, who often performs here weekends and during the full moon. By day it's the quintessential beach bar with BBQ ribs and grilled fresh seafood. At night there's a dance floor, beach bar, small menu, and potent rum cocktails, of course. In high season there's a $15 cover. ✉ *Rendezvous Bay* 📞 *264/497–6219* ⊕ *www.bankiebanx.net.*

★ Elvis' Beach Bar

BARS/PUBS | Actually a boat, this is a great place to hear music and sip the best rum punch on Earth. You can also snack on Mexican food (try the goat tacos), play beach volleyball, or watch football on the big TV. The bar is closed Tuesday, and there's live music Wednesday through Sunday nights in high season—plus food until 1 am. The full-moon LunaSea party doesn't disappoint. ⊠ *Sandy Ground Village* ☎ *264/772–0637.*

Johnno's Beach Stop

BARS/PUBS | Now operating Friday, Saturday, and Sunday after recovering from a 2018 fire, Johnno's offers live music and alfresco dancing and on Sunday afternoon, when just about everybody drops by, there's live jazz. This is *the* classic Caribbean beach bar, attracting a funky eclectic mix, from locals to movie stars. Johnno's continues to have a daytime lunch outpost on Prickly Pear Cay, with excellent snorkeling—it's a short boat trip from Sandy Ground. ⊠ *Sandy Ground Village* ☎ *264/476–5272.*

🛍 Shopping

Anguilla is by no means a shopping destination, but a couple of boutiques stock cute beachwear and accessories. Hard-core shopping enthusiasts might like a day trip to nearby St. Martin.

The island's tourist publication, *What We Do in Anguilla,* has shopping tips and is available free at the airport and in shops. For upscale designer sportswear, check out small boutiques in the larger resorts like the Four Seasons and CuisinArt. Outstanding local artists sell their work in galleries, which often arrange studio tours (or check with the Anguilla Tourist Board).

ART AND CRAFTS

Devonish Art Gallery

CRAFTS | This gallery purveys the wood, stone, and clay creations of Courtney Devonish, an internationally known potter and sculptor, plus creations by his wife, Carolle, a bead artist. Works by other Caribbean artists and regional antique maps are also available. ⊠ *West End Rd., George Hill* ☎ *264/497–2949* ⊕ *www.devonishart.com.*

Hibernia Restaurant and Art Gallery

ANTIQUES/COLLECTIBLES | Striking pieces are culled from the owners' travels, from contemporary Eastern European art to traditional Indo-Chinese crafts. ⊠ *Harbor Ridge Dr., Island Harbour* ☎ *264/497–4290* ⊕ *www.hiberniarestaurant.com* ☉ *Closed Mon. and mid-July–Nov. No lunch Sun.*

L. Bernbaum Art Gallery

ART GALLERIES | Originally from Texas, Lynne Bernbaum has been working and living in the Caribbean for more than 20 years and exhibits around the world. Her paintings and prints are inspired by the island's natural beauty but have unusual perspectives and a hint of surrealism. The gallery is open Monday through Saturday 4–8 pm. ⊠ *Sandy Ground Village* ☎ *264/497–5211* ⊕ *www. lynnebernbaum.com.*

Savannah Gallery

ART GALLERIES | Adjacent historic houses contain high-quality works by Anguillian artists; other contemporary Caribbean and Central American art, including oil paintings by Marge Morani; works from the renowned Haitian St. Soleil school; Guatemalan textiles; Mexican pottery; and Haitian metal sculpture, some made from recycled oil drums. ⊠ *Coronation St., Crocus Bay* ☎ *264/497–2263* ⊕ *www.savannahgallery.com* ⊘ *Closed Sun.*

CLOTHING

Caribbean Silkscreen

CLOTHING | Caribbean Silkscreen creates designs and prints island-theme golf shirts, hats, sweatshirts, and jackets. ⊠ *South Hill Village* ☎ *264/497–2272.*

Irie Life

CLOTHING | This popular boutique sells vividly hued beach and resort wear and flip-flops, as well as attractive handicrafts, jewelry, and collectibles from all over the Caribbean, many with a Rasta theme. ⊠ *South Hill Village* ☎ *264/497–6527* ⊕ *www.irielife.com.*

Limin' Boutique

JEWELRY/ACCESSORIES | Visit this attractive boutique for sensational repurposed jewelry and handicrafts such as iPad cases and wristlets made of old sails from Anguilla's famous racing boats, bracelets made from island musicians' discarded guitar strings, "Dune Jewelry" made from the sand from local beaches, and sea-salt body scrubs. There is also a good selection of stylish beach cover-ups. ⊠ *West End Main Rd., West End Village* ☎ *264/583–3733.*

Petals Boutique

CLOTHING | This lovely boutique has attractive beachwear, jewelry, and accessories, as well as an assortment of local products. ⊠ *Frangipani Beach Resort, Rte. 1, Long Bay Village* ☎ *264/497–6442* ⊘ *Closed Mon.*

SeaSpray Boutique and Smoothies

CRAFTS | Enjoy a rum punch or a fruit smoothie while you shop for Anguillian arts and crafts, handcrafted jewelry, and charming handmade Christmas ornaments. They stock delicious locally made preserves from Anguilla's Jammin and other souvenirs. ⊠ *South Hill Roundabout, The Valley* ☏ *264/235–1650.*

ZaZaa

CLOTHING | Sue Ricketts, the first lady of Anguilla marketing, owns three boutiques; on the Main Road in South Hill, near the entrance of Anacaona Boutique Hotel, on Meads Bay, and at the Shoal Bay Beach entrance. They carry Anguillian crafts; wonderful jewelry and beachwear, such as Brazilian bikinis and chic St. Barth goodies; and beach hats, sundries, and souvenirs. ⊠ *Lower South Hill, South Hill Village.*

🏃 Activities

Anguilla's expanding sports options include an excellent golf course (at the CuisinArt Golf Resort), designed by Greg Norman to accentuate the natural terrain and maximize the stunning ocean views over Rendezvous Bay. Players say the par-72 course is reminiscent of Pebble Beach. Personal experience says bring a lot of golf balls! The Anguilla Tennis Academy, designed by noted architect Myron Goldfinger, operates in the Blowing Point area. The 1,000-seat stadium, equipped with pro shop and seven lighted courts, was created to attract major international matches and to provide a first-class playing option for tourists and locals.

DIVING

Anguilla boasts seven marine park; sunken wrecks; a long barrier reef; walls, canyons, and hulking boulders; varied marine life, including greenback turtles and nurse sharks; and exceptionally clear water. All make for excellent diving. **Prickly Pear Cay** is a favorite spot. **Stoney Bay Marine Park,** off the northeast end, showcases the *El Buen Consejo,* a 960-ton Spanish galleon that sank in 1772. Divers love finding all 29 cannons. Other good dive sites include **Grouper Bowl,** with exceptional hard-coral formations; **Ram's Head,** with caves, chutes, and tunnels; and **Upper Flats,** where you are sure to see stingrays.

★ SCUBA SHACK - Shoal Bay Scuba and Watersports

BOATING | **FAMILY** | This highly rated PADI dive center runs up to six dives a day (closed Sunday) from two locations: at Roy's at Sandy Ground, and in West End. Dives with full equipment start at $130. There is a discount for multiday dives, and advanced courses are available. Snorkeling trips are available; daily snorkeling rentals are $20; weekly rate is $120. Numerous kids' programs and a PADI Jr. certification are available; the minimum age is 8 years old. The shop sells masks, snorkels, fins, T-shirts, hats, shorts, and SPF-50

A Day at the Boat Races

If you want a different kind of trip to Anguilla, try for a visit during Carnival, which usually starts on the first Monday in August and continues for about 10 days. Colorful parades, beauty pageants, music, delicious food, arts-and-crafts shows, fireworks, and nonstop partying are just the beginning. The music starts with sunrise jam sessions—as early as 4 am—and continues well into the night. The high point? The boat races. They are the national passion and the official national sport of Anguilla.

Anguillians from around the world return home to race old-fashioned,

made-on-the-island wooden boats that have been in use on the island since the early 1800s. Similar to some of today's fastest sailboats, these are 15 to 28 feet in length and sport only a mainsail and jib on a single 25-foot mast. The sailboats have no deck, so heavy bags of sand, boulders, and sometimes even people are used as ballast. As the boats reach the finish line, the ballast—including some of the sailors—gets thrown into the water in a furious effort to win the race. Spectators line the beaches and follow the boats on foot, by car, and from even more boats. You'll have almost as much fun watching the fans as you will the races.

water shirts. Private dives, snorkeling and sightseeing charters, private fishing charters, and sunset cruises are also offered. ⊠ *Sandy Ground Village* ☎ *264/235–1482.*

GOLF

★ CuisinArt Golf Resort

GOLF | This Greg Norman course, a $50 million wonder, qualifies as one of the best golf courses in the Caribbean. Thirteen of its 18 holes are directly on the water, and it features sweeping sea vistas, elevation changes, and an ecologically responsible watering system of ponds and lagoons that snake through the grounds. Players including President Bill Clinton have thrilled to the spectacular vistas of St. Maarten and blue sea at the tee box of the 390-yard starting hole—the Caribbean's answer to Pebble Beach. An attractive Italian restaurant serves lunch. The course typically closes the second half of October for maintenance. Dress requirements include long shorts or slacks and a collared shirt. ⊠ *Rendezvous Bay* ☎ *264/498–5602* ⊕ *www.cuisinartresort. com* ⊠ *$299 for 18 holes ($100 resort guests), $225 for 9 holes ($75 hotel guests)* 🏌 *18 holes, 7200 yards, par 72.*

GUIDED TOURS

A round-the-island tour by taxi takes about 2½ hours and costs about $55 for one or two people, $5 for each additional passenger. Special-interest nature and culture tours are available.

★ Bennie's Travel & Tours

TOUR—SPORTS | One of the island's more reliable tour operators also arranges private boat charters, event planning, real-estate tours, and personal security services. ⊠ *Blowing Point Village* ☎ *264/497–2788* ⊕ *www.benniestravel.com.*

Nature Explorers Anguilla

ECOTOURISM | **FAMILY** | Ecotourists, photographers, families, and bird-watchers can enjoy a variety of tours of Anguilla's wildlife and wetlands. Tours can be customized by age of the group and interests, and range in time and price. Pickup is at your hotel or villa. Tours include use of binoculars, guidebooks, and bottled water. They also offer a seven-day/six-night tour package. ☎ *264/584–0346* ⊕ *natureexplorersanguilla.com* ⊠ *From $50.*

HORSEBACK RIDING

Seaside Stables

HORSEBACK RIDING | **FAMILY** | Ever dreamed of a sunset gallop (or slow clomp) on the beach? A bareback ocean romp is roughly $125, private rides any time of day are about $90 per hour, and morning and afternoon group rides are around $75. Prior riding experience is not required, as the horses are very gentle. Choose from English, Western, or Australian saddles. ⊠ *Paradise Dr., Cove Bay* ☎ *264/235–3667* ⊕ *www.seaside-stables.com* ⊠ *$90 private ride, $75 group ride.*

SEA EXCURSIONS

A number of boating options are available for airport transfers, day trips to offshore cays or neighboring islands, night trips to St. Martin, or just whipping through the waves en route to a picnic spot.

Calypso Charters

BOATING | Book a private or semiprivate charter with Calypso on one of their five powerboats for a trip around Anguilla, a fishing trip, or a sea excursion to St. Barth, St. Maarten, or the surrounding islands. They offer a lovely two-hour sunset cruise leaving from Cole Bay every Tuesday and Thursday. They also provide airport transfers. ⊠ *Sandy Ground Village* ☎ *264/584–8504* ⊕ *www.calypsochartersanguilla.com.*

Funtime Charters

BOATING | With five powerboats from 32 to 38 feet, this charter and shuttle service arranges private and scheduled boat transport to the airport, including luggage services ($70 per person one way for adults); day trips to St. Barth; and other powerboat excursions. The air-conditioned 42-seat *Sunshine Express* runs to SXM in the late night and early morning, as well as interisland excursions. ⊠ *Cove Bay* ☎ *264/497–6511* ⊕ *www.funtimecharters.com.*

★ Junior's Glass Bottom Boat

DIVING/SNORKELING | **FAMILY** | Junior has a great reputation for showing you the underwater scenery of Anguilla, starting with reef trips on his glass bottom boat. For an underwater peek at sea turtles and stingrays without getting wet, catch a ride on this boat. Guided snorkeling trips and instruction are available, too; Junior is great with kids and very knowledgeable. It's best to book in advance, especially during holidays. Hotel transport is available. His services are $40–$80 per person per hour depending on what you'd like to do; children 7 years and under are free. ⊠ *Shoal Bay Village* ☎ *264/235–1008* ⊕ *www.junior.ai.*

Sandy Island Enterprises

BOATING | Picnic, swimming, and diving excursions to Prickly Pear Cay, Sandy Island, and Scilly Cay are available through this outfit, which also rents Sunfish and windsurfers and arranges fishing charters. The Sandy Island sea shuttle *Happiness* leaves from the small pier in Sandy Ground daily November through August and by reservation in September and October. ⊠ *Sandy Ground Village* ☎ *264/497–6534* ⊕ *www.mysandyisland.com* ☞ *Open by reservation only Sept. 1–Oct. 31.*

Surf AXA

SURFING | Surf AXA offers everything for beginner or experienced surfers and paddleboarders, including instruction and rentals. They offer guided surf tours, too. ECO land tours and stand-up paddleboard rentals are now available. ⊠ *South Hill Village* ☎ *264/583–4613* ⊕ *surfaxa.com* ☜ *$20/hr or $50/day surfboard rental; $25/hr or $60/day stand-up paddleboard rental.*

INDEX

PHOTO CREDITS

Front Cover: Jerome Louden [Description: High angle view of people enjoying in sea against cliff, Anguilla.] **Back cover, from left to right:** Sean Pavone/Shutterstock, Maridav/Shutterstock, Steve Heap/Shutterstock. **Spine:** mfron/iStockphoto. **Interior, from left to right:** Sean Pavone/Shutterstock (1). daniloforcellini /iStockphoto (2). **Chapter 1: Experience St. Maarten, St. Barth, and Anguilla:** Photostravellers/Shutterstock (6-7). thierrydehove.com (8). Courtesy of Tainos & Kalinas Perles (9). Loterie Farm (9). Grand Case Lolo Grill by Richie Diesterheft (10). Zach Stovall (10). nik wheeler/Alamy (10). Ribe/Dreamstime (11). Martin Wheeler III/Shutterstock (12). Nikolay Tranov/Shutterstock (12). thierrydehove. com/CuisinArt Resort & Spa (12). SeanPavonePhoto/istockphoto (13). Olivier Goujon/agefotostock (13). Slim Plantagenate /Alamy (14). DIDIER FORRAY/ age fotostock (14). Courtesy_Hotel Le Toiny Restauran (14). Sean Pavone/shutterstock (15). Kristopher Kettner/Shutterstock (18). daniloforcellini/iStockphoto (18). Malachi Jacobs/Shutterstock (18). Eq Roy/Dreamstime (18). mtcurado/ iStockphoto (19). Courtesy of Replay Restaurant & Bar (20). Courtesy of Vesna Taverna (21). Courtesy of Tainos & Kalinas Perles (22). Vesna Taverna (23). **Chapter 3: St. Maarten/St. Martin:** SpVVK/istockphoto (53). Sean Pavone/Shutterstock (88). Steve Heap/Shutterstock (93). bcampbell65/shutterstock (102). Chris Floyd (104). **Chapter 4: St. Barthélemy:** Sean Pavone/istockphoto (105). Christian Wheatley/iStockphoto (111). Leonard Zhukovsky/Shutterstock (123). Joe Benning/Shutterstock (126). Restaurant Le Gaiac (131). Photostravellers/ Shutterstock (138). **Chapter 5: Anguilla:** Chris Caldicott/agefotostock (145). Rick Strange/agefotostock (156). Straw Hat (164). The Leading Hotels of the World (168). **All photos are courtesy of the writers.**

*Every effort has been made to trace the copyright holders, and we apologize in advance for any accidental errors. We would be happy to apply the corrections in the following edition of this publication.

NOTES

NOTES

NOTES

NOTES

NOTES

NOTES

NOTES